W9-ALV-582

DISCARD

The German-American Heritage

Irene M. Franck

Part of the America's Ethnic Heritage series
General Editors: David M. Brownstone and Irene M. Franck

Facts On File
New York • Oxford

The German-American Heritage

Library of Congress Cataloging-in-Publication Data

Franck, Irene M.
The German-American heritage / by Irene M. Franck.
p. cm. — (America's ethnic heritage)
Bibliography: p.
Includes index.
Summary: Explores the history, culture, and contributions of
German-Americans from colonial times to the present.
ISBN 0-8160-1629-1
1. German Americans—History—Juvenile literature. [1. German
Americans—History.] I. Title. II. Series.
E184.G3F76 1988   88-16417
973'.0431—dc19

British CIP data available on request

Printed in the United States of America

10 9 8 7 6 5 4 3 2 1

Contents

Preface

The German-American Heritage is a volume in the *America's Ethnic Heritage* series, which explores the unique background of each of America's ethnic groups—their history and culture, their reasons for leaving home, their long journey to America, their waves of settlement in the new land, their often-difficult years of adjustment as they made their way into the American mainstream, and their contributions to the overall society we call "America."

We would like to thank the many people who helped us in completing this work: our expert typists, Shirley Fenn and Mary Racette; Domenico Firmani, photo researcher *par excellence*; skilled cartographer Dale Adams; James Warren, our excellent editor at Facts On File; his very able assistant, Barbara Levine; publisher Edward Knappman, who supported the series from the start; and the many fine members of the Facts On File editorial and production staff.

We also express our special appreciation to the many librarians whose help has been indispensable in completing this work, especially to the incomparable staff of the Chappaqua Library—director Mark Hasskari; the reference staff, including Mary Platt, Paula Peyraud, Terry Cullen, Martha Alcott, and Carolyn Jones; Jane McKean, Caroline Chojnowski, and formerly Marcia Van Fleet and the whole circulation staff—and the many other librarians who, through the Interlibrary Loan network, have provided us with the research tools so vital to our work.

Irene M. Franck
David M. Brownstone

America's Ethnic Heritage

The United States is a great sea of peoples. All the races, nations, and beliefs of the world are met here. We live together, joined with each other while at the same time keeping our own separate identities. And it works. Sometimes there is pain and struggle for equality and justice, but it works—and will continue to work for as long as we all want it to.

We have brought with us to America all the ethnic heritages of the world. In that respect, there is no other place like this on earth—no other place where all the histories of all the peoples come together. Some have therefore called the United States a great "melting pot." But that is not quite right. We do not mix and completely merge our ethnic heritages. Instead we mix them, partially merge them, and at the same time keep important parts of them whole. The result is something unique called an American.

1

The German-Americans

What do Fred Astaire, millionaire fur trader John Jacob Astor, baseball great Babe Ruth, actress-singer Marlene Dietrich, Revolutionary War hero Baron Friedrich von Steuben, oil tycoon John D. Rockefeller, children's book author Dr. Seuss, and President Dwight D. Eisenhower have in common? They are all German-Americans.

In fact, perhaps one out of every five Americans has some German ancestry. No other people, except the British, sent more immigrants to America's shores. The German contributions to American life fit those numbers. The Germans come from a proud culture and brought with them to America many extraordinary intellectual, scientific, and artistic gifts. And much that we regard today as simply "American"—everything from the Christmas tree and the Easter bunny to hamburgers and frankfurters to Tootsie Rolls and Hershey bars—sprang from the culture of German-American immigrants.

Gifts to America

The German-Americans are a strongly religious people. They are, first of all, the people of the great Protestant leader Martin Luther. The Protestant religion, which has been so important in America, started in Germany. More than that, many German-Americans were and are firm believers in religious tolerance. Germany itself has often been noted for religions *in*tolerance—from the bitter Protestant-Catholic wars of the 16th and 17th centuries to the terrible massacre of millions of Jews in the 20th century. But many German-Americans left Germany precisely because of religious wars. In this country, many held fast to their religious beliefs and have often fought for religious freedom.

The German-Americans are also the people of Johann Gutenberg. In mid-15th-century Germany, he developed the process of printing, which revolutionized the modern world. German cities became major centers of learning, with many scholars, writers, publishing houses, and universities. Music, too, flourished in Germany, giving the world great composers like Mozart, Beethoven, Bach, and many others. Coming from this background, German-Americans made huge contributions to the cultural and intellectual life of the growing United States. They founded many of the most important music organizations in America and helped shape modern American education, from the kindergarten to the university graduate schools.

The Germans are also the people of the great physicist Albert Einstein. He and many other Germans brought valuable scientific and technical skills to America. The famous Kentucky rifle was created by German-American gunsmiths; the covered "Conestoga" wagon used by so many westbound pioneers was first built by German-American wagonmakers; the amazing Brooklyn Bridge suspension system was designed by a German-American engineer; and the rockets that took Americans to the moon were developed largely by German rocket scientists.

The Germans are also the people of Europe's 1848 revolutions, so they brought with them a great love of political freedom and democracy. Germany itself has often been ruled by dictators, but many of the German people favored democracy. Despairing of democratic reform at home, large numbers of them came to join in the great democracy of the United States. Many German-Americans had strong feelings against slavery.

Baseball legend Babe Ruth, one of the most famous and best-loved athletes of the 20th century, was a Baltimore-born German-American. (Library of Congress)

They felt it was morally wrong and against the American ideal of freedom for all. They produced the first formal protest against slavery in America, in 1688, and were active in founding the anti-slavery Republican Party in the mid-19th century. As the Civil War approached, they helped sway American public opinion toward the anti-slavery Union. No less a figure than Abraham Lincoln said that the Germans ". . . are more enthusiastic for the cause of Freedom than all the other nationalities."

The Germans are also the people of the plow. Tens of thousands of German immigrants came from farms in Europe to farms in America. And they are a traveling people, too. For centuries, they migrated over Europe. In America, they formed a major part of the westward movement, first helping to settle the frontier lands of the colonies, and then pushing westward through the Appalachian Mountains into Ohio and Kentucky and out to the Mississippi River. Later many settled in the Great Plains that form the heartland of the United States. In all these regions they opened up new land to farming and helped found many of the major towns and cities of mid-America.

Since the discovery of America, millions of Germans—perhaps seven million, or even more—have left Europe to settle in the United States. Yet for all their numbers, and for the great contributions they have made to the United States, it is hard to say precisely who the "Germans" are.

The Wanderers

Before the founding of the German Empire in 1871, no single country called "Germany" existed. Germanic Europe was only a patchwork quilt of tiny states. There certainly were people we would call Germans (they called themselves *Deutsch*), but their common bond lay in their language, culture, customs, and heritage, not in a fully unified political history. Noted German-American historian Hajo Holborn put it this way:

> Germany cannot be described in clear-cut geographical terms.
> During more than a thousand years the boundaries of Germany
> have continuously and drastically changed, as have the areas
> settled by Germans. Usually Germany is simply said to be the
> country in the center of the European continent.

Even after the formation of the German Empire, many "Germans" were found far beyond its borders. People who spoke German, practiced

German traditions and customs, worshipped in German-style churches, and thought of themselves as *Deutsch* lived in many parts of Europe, including Switzerland, Russia, Poland, Austria, Hungary, Czechoslovakia, and the Netherlands.

Much has been written in modern times about the pull of the German "Fatherland" or "Rhineland," meaning the lands along the Rhine River. But, in fact, Germanic peoples have been wandering the globe for thousands of years, always seeking greener pastures. Their language even has a word for these great migrations: *Völkerwanderung* (folk-wandering). They have a word, too, for the desire to seek adventure through travel: *Wanderlust*.

By the time of Christ, the Germanic peoples had started spreading over much of Europe. In later centuries, whole groups of these peoples would uproot themselves from one place in Europe and migrate to another. The migration to America was part of this long-term historical pattern. Given that history, it is no surprise that many Germans headed for the frontier in America, moving ever farther westward, until the frontier finally closed around the end of the 19th century.

The people of Germany were also used to migrating with the seasons, looking for work. These were not, generally, people who lived in one place and never ventured beyond their village borders. Quite the contrary. Many of the people who came to America from the Germanic states had only recently settled into homes in the Rhineland—they had come either from more easterly Germanic states or from other parts of Europe. Moving was nothing new for them.

To complicate matters further, individual German states were sometimes havens for people from other parts of Europe. Religious, political, and economic refugees, among them Jews, Poles, Dutch, French, Scandinavians, Russians, Swiss, Italians, and even English have at times looked to various German states for new homes. Sometimes these immigrants would stay for a short time and move on. Other immigrants stayed for generations. Many French Protestants, for example, fled to Germany during the Catholic-Protestant wars of the 16th century. Later, when some of their descendants emigrated to America, they were seen as simply "German." Large numbers of Jews also came to German states, as traders or refugees. By the 19th century many of them had lived there so long that they considered themselves simply "Germans." That would bring disaster in the 20th century, when the Nazis came to power.

Many people who came from the German states, then, had originally come from a different cultural background. So, in looking at the German contribution to American life, it is sometimes difficult to tell simply who is a German.

Who Are the Germans?

In this book we will take a very broad view of the Germans. Some immigration figures, such as those of the U.S. Bureau of the Census, count as Germans only those people who were born in the territory of the German Empire, later the German Republic. Some others consider "Germans" to be anyone who lived in any of the states that eventually went to make up the German Empire, but not anyone living elsewhere in Europe.

But in a wider sense, "Germans" are all those people who consider themselves so, by history or culture, regardless of changing political boundaries. That includes many people from lands outside of "Germany" proper. Sometimes these Germans had not moved at all, but had had political boundaries change around them. That was true, for example, in

Fred Astaire—who created a uniquely American dance style that brought pleasure to millions of people all over the world—was Kansas-born, the son of an Austrian-American brewer.
(Copyright Washington Post; reprinted by permission of the D.C. Public Library)

Switzerland, Austria, Poland, and Alsace-Lorraine, the disputed borderlands between Germany and France. Some Germans had long ago moved to distant lands, notably Russia, but kept their language and culture, as many would do in America.

In this book we will consider all of these people to be "Germans" and we will explore their history and their many contributions to American life.

2

The Old Country

The German people lived in some of the most attractive lands in Europe, including many fertile river valleys. Most important of these rivers is the Rhine, which flows from the high Alps down to the North Sea. As German-American historian La Vern Rippley put it, an "imaginary giant" standing in the Alps facing the Rhine would see "a staircase descending to the sea." The valleys of the Rhine and its main feeder rivers—the Main, the Neckar, and the Ruhr—formed the heart of Germany in the late Middle Ages. This is Germany's famous "Rhineland" or "Fatherland."

But in centuries of eastward expansion, other rivers also played an important role in German history. To the east of the Rhine are the Weser, the Elbe, and the Oder, all major waterways flowing from the Alps to the North or Baltic seas. Angling eastward from the Alps toward the Black Sea is the Danube River. The Danube's headwaters, if not its lower reaches, lie firmly in Germanic territory.

The heartland of Germany is something like eastern North America, where many early German immigrants settled. Valleys like the Hudson and the Ohio have much in common with the valleys of the Rhine, the Danube, and the Elbe. Along the lower and middle reaches of these rivers lie prime flat farmlands. Even the upper reaches, in hilly country, are often fertile and productive. The foliage, too, is similar. The same kinds of leafy trees—maples, oaks, beeches, elms, ashes, and the like—grow among the low hills. Firs are more common in the higher mountains, as in the famous Black Forest of Germany, which lies in the Alps around the headwaters of the Rhine and Danube rivers. Europe's Alps are higher than America's eastern mountain chain, the Appalachians, but the soil and the climate are somewhat similar. All of these similarities gave German farmers a distinct advantage in America, because the crops, livestock, and farming methods of the old country readily translated to the new.

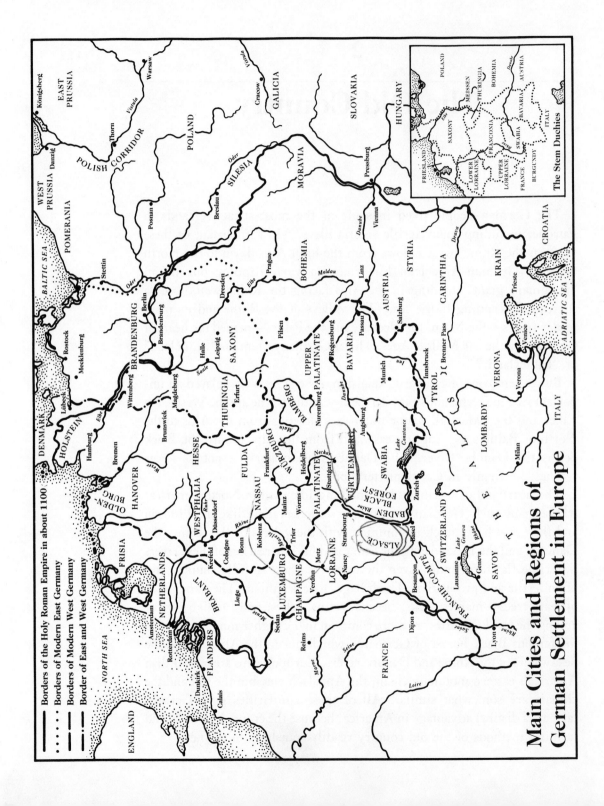

Main Cities and Regions of German Settlement in Europe

The Indo-Europeans

The German people have not always lived in Northern Europe. Like most of their neighbors, they came to Europe from elsewhere. But exactly where they came from and when we do not know for certain.

We do know that the Germans are one of the many related peoples of Eurasia. Their cousins today live and rule in such distant countries as Spain and Greece, Norway and Iran, Russia and India. All these peoples and many more shared a common language and culture many thousands of years ago. They were such successful conquerors that they took most of Eurasia, from India to far Scandinavia.

As a result, their language and culture are today called "Indo-European." A century ago these people were commonly called "Aryans." But in the 20th century Hitler's Nazis adopted the term "Aryan" to refer to the so-called "pure" Germans, who were supposed to be superior to all other peoples of the world. That was all nonsense, of course. In fact, no people is "pure." Human groups have mixed with each other all over the world for many thousands of years.

Over many centuries, the Indo-European-speaking peoples gradually divided into groups distinguished by somewhat different language and culture. The Germanic peoples pushed their Indo-European cousins, the Celts, westward before them and came to dominate in Northern Europe.

Roman Times

The great Roman general Julius Caesar respected the strength and courage of Northern Europe's Germanic tribes. His *Gallic Wars*, written in the first century B.C., contains one of the earliest references to them. Caesar and his legions took Gaul (now modern France) and conquered some Germanic tribes who lived west of the Rhine River. But neither he nor other Roman leaders had much success against the Germanic peoples east of the Rhine and north of the Danube. Hermann, leader of the tribes who stopped the Romans in 9 A.D., is celebrated as a great German hero.

In the end the Romans settled for building a great line of fortifications, called the *Limes*, between the Roman Empire and the region they called Germania. Begun in 84 A.D., the Limes ran across Europe for hundreds of miles, roughly following the line of the lower Rhine River and the smaller Neckar River, then crossing through the Alps to follow the Danube River to its mouth.

The Limes ran on the eastern bank of the Rhine, so Roman civilization came very early to the western part of the Rhineland. Roman citizens brought to the region temples to the various Roman gods, Jewish synagogues, and later Christian churches. The Romans planted vineyards, the beginnings of the fine wines of the Rhine and Moselle valleys. They also brought their excellent talents in administration and their higher technology to the region. All of these would much influence the Germans of later times.

Some of the great cities of modern Germany grew up around major Roman trading towns or forts, especially along the Limes. In the north, along the lower Rhine, the main center was Colonia Agrippina; that became modern Cologne. In the middle Rhine, the provincial center was Moguntiacum, now the city of Mainz. The Roman town of Augusta Treverorum became today's Trier. It was there that Constantine was proclaimed emperor of Rome. He was the emperor who, in the fourth century A.D., made Christianity the official religion of all the empire. Bonn, the present capital of West Germany, also has Roman roots, as do many other cities west of the Rhine-Danube line, including Strasbourg, Augsburg, Regensburg, Koblenz, Linz, and Vienna.

From the first to the third centuries A.D., while Rome was strong, the Limes largely kept the Germanic tribes east of the frontier. But as Rome weakened in the fourth and fifth centuries, the Germanic tribes began to pour through the old Limes into Western Europe. They moved into northwestern lowlands, spread over Gaul, invaded Spain, and even occupied Italy. Some of the kingdoms they founded lasted only a short time, such as those of the Goths and the Vandals. But others remained to form some of the countries of modern Europe. A Germanic tribe called the Franks, for example, settled in—and gave their name to—France. The Angles and Saxons, from Europe's northwestern lowlands, crossed the sea to the southeastern British Isles. Their land came to be known as Angleland—or England.

New Empires

The Germanic peoples saw themselves as heirs to the Roman Empire. At first, the many tribes divided Europe into separate kingdoms. But by the late eighth century, one tribe—the Franks—became strong enough to unite them. The man responsible for this feat was the Frankish king Charlemagne (Charles the Great). In the year 800 A.D., he traveled to the city of Rome, where the pope crowned him "Emperor of the Romans."

Charlemagne's empire at that time stretched from Spain to the North Sea, and from the Baltic Sea south to include much of Central Europe, over half of Italy, and everything in between. It was a massive empire, but after Charlemagne's death in 814, it quickly fell apart into smaller kingdoms.

The Franks remained in what is now France. Smaller tribes remained in regions such as Friesland (now the Netherlands) and Burgundy (today divided between France and Switzerland), as well as across the sea in England and Scandinavia. The other Germanic tribes centered around the Rhine gradually grouped themselves into five main duchies (small states), which they called *Stamms* (stems). These stem duchies were: Saxony in the north, Franconia in the center, Bavaria to the southeast, Swabia to the southwest, and Lorraine to the west. The Rhine passes through the western parts of Franconia and Swabia; many of the early German immigrants to America would come from these regions.

After the fall of the Roman Empire, Charlemagne, king of the franks, united the German tribes and declared himself "Roman Emperor."
(After an engraving by Giuseppe Longhi, Library of Congress)

But the idea of empire lived. In 911 the Germans in the five stem duchies selected a king, a *regnum Teutonicum*. ("Teutonic" is another word for German.) Then in 962 Otto the Great, a Saxon elected as German king, followed Charlemagne's example and went to Rome. There the pope crowned him "Emperor of the Romans."

Otto I's "Roman Empire" was smaller than Charlemagne's, but it was still large. Generally it was bounded in the west by the Rhine and in the east by the Elbe and Salle rivers. This new "Roman Empire" would survive, with many changes in its borders, until 1806. In the 12th century it also received a new name: The Holy Roman Empire of the German nation. Many historians consider the crowning of Otto the beginning of "Germany."

The young, loosely organized empire had little unity, however. The five stem duchies operated as relatively independent states. (Even today, some regional variations in dialect and culture survive from these centuries-old tribal divisions.) By the 13th century the stem duchies themselves had fragmented into many smaller states. Many of the castles that still mark Germany's landscape were built in these centuries, by princes or knights anxious to retain their own small lands in the endless struggles with each other and the emperor. The name "The Holy Roman Empire" was always more a dream than reality.

The name does, however, indicate the Germans' close relationship with the Catholic Church of Rome. Charlemagne had brought Christianity eastward across the Rhine River into Saxony in the late eighth and early ninth centuries. Many of Germany's "Roman emperors" became so involved in church affairs in Italy that they paid little attention to their empire. The power of the "Holy Roman Emperor" was, then, quite limited in practice.

Many German cities also became independent and self-ruling, especially under the Hohenstaufen line of emperors in the 12th and 13th centuries. Apart from paying annual taxes to the emperor, these cities' inhabitants were free citizens, owing no allegiance to any prince. Much of the German population in the countryside was caught in the bonds of serfdom. Peasants were tied to the land of their overlords, almost like slaves. But serfdom had no place in these cities. Not surprisingly, city dwellers felt that: "City air is free air."

By the late 13th century, the German princes had asserted some control over the cities. Even so, these free cities gave Germany a special character. They acted against political unity, while promoting economic growth.

Push to the East

Even before Otto I was crowned Roman emperor, the Germans had begun what would be a thousand-year-long expansion. East of the Elbe River lay the lightly populated plains of Northern Europe, held by Slavic peoples. Weakened by attacks from their east, the Slavs were easy prey for the Germans.

Otto himself led the Germans into the Austrian lands, to the present-day border of Hungary on the Leith River. Bavarian and Franconian settlers quickly spread down the Danube River into Austria, overcoming the Slavic peoples. Germans also settled in Bohemia (part of modern Czechoslovakia), expanded northward into the province of Holstein (at the base of modern Denmark), and followed the Brenner Pass through the Alps into northern Italy.

But the main German push was eastward across the Elbe River. From the 10th century on, Germans from all five stem duchies pushed beyond the Elbe, gradually conquering and settling the borderlands, called *marches*. They did not always have immediate success. Though they crossed the Oder River within decades of Otto's crowning, the local Slavs often revolted, notably in 982, and temporarily held off full German settlement of the marches. But gradually, between 1150 and 1350, these marches were made part of the Holy Roman Empire.

German expansion was often violent. Spurred on by the Catholic Church, they sometimes went after the "heathen"—that is, non-Christian—Slavs with murderous crusading zeal. Among the Crusaders were a German military-religious order called the Teutonic Knights. Long active Crusaders in the Mediterranean, these Teutonic Knights were brought to the northeastern coastland of Prussia in the early 13th century. There, with the blessings of the Catholic Church and the Polish rulers, they killed most of the Slavic tribe called the Prussians. Then they settled down to rule over the region from their capital at Königsberg (today Kaliningrad), on the Baltic Sea. Not surprisingly, the Slavs harbored bitter feelings against these German invaders.

But elsewhere Germans sometimes moved in without major opposition or bloodshed. They were even, in some areas, almost welcomed, for they brought a higher technology and standard of living to some rather backward lands. Better tools allowed them to clear forested land more efficiently and farm it more effectively. In coastal or boggy lands, they successfully employed Frisian (Dutch) methods of draining swamps and building dikes. Germans also brought with them expert skills in various industrial crafts, such as mining. With their urban experience stretching back to Roman times, these German colonists founded and developed many of the towns and cities in the marches east of the Elbe River.

The new territories beyond the Elbe and down the Danube formed "colonial Germany." In these frontier lands, many Germans found freedom and opportunities not open to them in the stem duchies. The Slavs and other peoples in many of the colonial territories were overpowered and largely submerged. The German settlers from the various stem duchies gradually lost their regional dialects and customs. In the end many of these areas came to be considered simply "German."

Jews in Germany

Though the German states were largely Christian, Jewish communities had remained and grown since Roman times, especially along the Rhine, in cities like Cologne. Christians carried many deep-rooted prejudices against the Jews. They forced them to live in *ghettoes,* which were segregated Jews-only sections of medieval cities. Barred by law from farming and many professions and crafts, many Jews made their living as traders and financiers. Although Charlemagne had given Jews some modest protection, in later centuries anti-Jewish activities were common.

This was especially so during the time of the Crusades, starting in 1096. The Crusaders, many of them German knights and peasants, headed for the Middle East. They were aiming to fight the Moslem Turks, who refused to allow Christian visits to the Holy Land. But on their way the Crusaders slaughtered tens of thousands of Jews in cities such as Metz, Worms, and Prague.

Over the next four centuries, German Jews would be subject to many other massacres, by Crusaders and by local peoples. They were blamed for everything from Mongol attacks to periodic plagues. In 1298 Jews were expelled from the Holy Roman Empire. Not all left, or some returned, for they were expelled from the Empire again in 1348 and from Austria in 1421. Many of the German Jews fled eastward into Polish lands.

Germany and Its Neighbors

By the 14th century, Poland was Germany's main rival to the east. This rising Slavic kingdom was centered between the Oder and Vistula rivers.

At the Battle of Tannenberg in 1410, the Poles defeated the Teutonic Knights, winning from them the Vistula River Valley. Because this gave the Poles an important pathway to the Baltic Sea, it was named the "Polish Corridor." This Polish Corridor cut East Prussia off from Western Prussia and the rest of the German states and set the stage for centuries of confict between the Germans and the Poles.

With the rise of Poland, the migration of German farmers and merchants was diverted in other directions, especially to Bohemia (in modern Czechoslovakia) and the rich mining region of Silesia, along the upper Oder River. German settlers brought to these regions their considerable skills in agriculture, industrial crafts, business, and military activities. As elsewhere, they established many towns and cities.

While Silesia came heavily under German influence, Bohemia resisted it. The Bohemian kings encouraged German settlement in the 13th century, but the local Czech population resented the Germans. When the Czechs gained control of Bohemia in the 15th century, they barred Germans from holding government or church offices. The Germans turned the tables in the 16th century, when the Austrian Hapsburg rulers took Bohemia. This conflict, too, would continue to echo into the 20th century.

In the 13th and 14th centuries, the German states were also faced with rising powers to their west, notably France and Burgundy. The Hundred Years' War with England turned France's attention elsewhere in the following century, but the western German states still lost some territory to France. The long conflict between France and Germany over the borderlands of Alsace and Lorraine would extend into modern times.

The Holy Roman Empire

Over the centuries, the Holy Roman Emperor and the various princely and church officials continued to struggle for power. In 1356, the powers resolved some of their differences in the Golden Bull, an agreement named for its gold seal. This specified who had a vote in electing the emperor, with the pope's blessing. Among these privileged few *electors* were the rulers of Saxony, Bohemia, Brandenburg (the eastern region around modern Berlin), the "count palatine" of the Rhine, and the archbishops of Mainz, Cologne, and Trier. The count's territory, known as the Palatinate, later sent many German immigrants to America. Major areas had no electors, however, including Bavaria and Austria. That left

The Holy Roman Emperor was elected by princes and priests, and had always to worry about pleasing them and keeping their support. (By Jost Amman, from *The Book of Trades*, late 16th century)

many dukes and knights with no voice in choosing the emperor they were supposed to serve—a sure recipe for trouble.

The Holy Roman Emperor only became a powerful figure after the mid-15th century, when Austria's Hapsburg dynasty came to the imperial throne. A series of carefully planned marriages brought the Hapsburgs part of Burgundy (the rest went to France), Luxembourg, and the Netherlands. Through later marriages, the Hapsburgs would gain the thrones of Spain, Naples, Sicily, and, in the end, Bohemia and Hungary. First elected to the German imperial throne in 1438, the Hapsburgs formed a hereditary dynasty that would rule the Holy Roman Empire until 1806, with just a three-year break in the 18th century.

The Free Cities

In the late 14th century Europe was hit by a terrible plague—the Black Death—which killed as many as one out of every four Germans. Cities and towns were emptied; land went unplowed; migration to the east halted. After the Black Death, much changed in daily life. Many survivors left the land for the cities, where they could have more individual freedom and a richer life. Those who stayed on the land were able to gain somewhat more rights and money, too, since their labor was more necessary and valued.

In the years of recovery, many German cities banded together and took the lead in developing new commerce and industry, though German princes tried to stop them. These cities joined in a great commercial federation called the Hanseatic League. The string of Hanseatic trading cities ran along the coast of the North and Baltic seas, from the Netherlands to East Prussia, including parts of Scandinavia and Russia as well. Prime among the German Hanseatic cities were the headquarters city, Lübeck, east of the Danish peninsula, and Hamburg, west of Denmark.

The Hanseatic League's trading network eventually stretched from the North and Baltic seas across the Alps to Italy and on across the Mediterranean to the Middle East. Herring, grain, wine, textiles, metals, and industrial and agricultural products of all sorts were exchanged through German traders—this despite the fact that tolls and taxes were collected along the way by each German state.

The largest German city around 1500 was the commercial hub in this trading network: Augsburg, in southern Germany. Many of Europe's most powerful financial and trading companies had their offices there. With nearly 50,000 people, Augsburg had by this time surpassed the size of the second-largest city, Cologne, a major silk-weaving center. Nuremberg, also in the south, had about 30,000 people; so did Magdeburg, on the Elbe River.

The cities became an increasingly striking feature of Germany. They were centers of commerce and industry. Many city dwellers became skilled artisans, forming craft guilds to oversee the quality and quantity of their work. In the cities, leading merchants and guild members came to rank on a par with the once-dominant nobles and actively participated in city government.

Cities were also centers of education and culture, quite unlike the countryside. In 1348, the Holy Roman Emperor founded the first German university, in Prague. When Czech religious reformers called the Hussites (followers of John Huss) drove the Germans out of Prague, the scholars created a new university at Leipzig, in 1409. In between those two dates, universities were founded at Vienna, Heidelberg, Cologne, and Erfurt. Others followed in the 15th and 16th centuries, notably at Trier, Basel, Mainz, and Wittenberg.

These universities focused very much on religion, medicine, and the law. Students studied in Latin and Greek and, in the study of the Bible, Hebrew as well. Much religious scholarship was aimed at a deeper understanding of Christianity and a moral revival in the church. This helped prepare the way for the great religious upheaval known as the Reformation.

The German universities were at first somewhat limited, but through contact with the Italian Renaissance, they were soon making major contributions. Johann Müller, better known by his Latin name of Regiomantanus, laid the basis for a mathematical view of the universe. Astronomer Johannes Kepler described in mathematical terms the movement of the planets around the sun. Paracelsus (born von Hohenheim), working at the University of Basel, transformed pharmacy, making chemical drugs where once only herbal medicines had been used. They and others like them set the stage for the later flowering of scholarship and science of modern Germany. The late 15th and early 16th centuries also saw some of Germany's greatest painters, including Albrect Dürer, from Nuremberg, and Hans Holbein the Younger, who left his home in Swabia to work largely in England.

It was in this period that the Germans made a revolutionary contribution to the Western world: Johann Gutenberg developed the process of printing with movable type. Gutenberg himself worked as a printer in Mainz for no more than 10 years, between about 1450 and 1460. But other printers—recognizing the importance of his invention—gathered in Mainz, making it a literary center. From there they spread out around Germany. By 1500 printers were operating in over 60 German towns and cities. The great thinkers of Europe flocked to German cities to have their works printed. So German cities came to be in the forefront of the new ideas of education and scholarship in Europe.

Changing Times

The power of the Hanseatic League fueled endless struggles, however. Princes tried to assert control over the cities. In the decades after the Black Death, the rule of law broke down in many parts of Germany, resulting in feuds and civil wars. Religious divisions within the Roman Catholic Church threatened both the papacy and the empire. Church inquisitors conducted widespread witch trials in the mid-15th century.

In the north and east, princes were often more powerful than either church or city officials. Most powerful was the Order of the Teutonic Knights in East Prussia. During the 15th century, two northern states became increasingly dominant in the empire. One was Saxony, with its important metal and salt mines, and the other Brandenburg, centered around Berlin and ruled by the Hohenzollern dynasty.

After Johann Gutenberg invented printing from movable type in Mainz, German printers made their country an intellectual center of Europe.
(By Jost Amman, from *The Book of Trades*, late 16th century)

At the beginning of the 16th century, "Germany" had more people and territory than any other country in Europe. Its 20 million people were concentrated most densely in the Rhine Valley, least densely east of the Elbe. In some areas of the southwest, notably Alsace, Swabia, and Bavaria, little farmland was available.

Three-quarters of Germany's population in the 16th century worked at farming. In the old stem duchies, land was mostly in the hands of the nobles or the church. In the lowlands of Friesland and Holstein and in the Alpine areas of Tyrol and the Black Forest, some peasants held their own land, probably because they had drained or cleared it themselves.

Most peasants, however, worked land owned by others. In medieval times, such peasants had been bound to their landlords by a whole web of legal bonds and obligations. Gradually—especially after the Black Death—these bonds were being broken. But in the process the peasants sometimes lost their rights to remain on the land and to pass those rights on to their children. Instead they could be thrown off at the lord's pleasure.

Calls for Reform

In 16th-century Germany, dukes and princes sparred with each other, with the emperor, and with the church for power. On a local level this led to wide-scale confusion. Peasants could be answerable to several sets of authorities, with one controlling the land they worked, another imposing legal obligations for service, and another dispensing justice in the region.

Such a system suited no one very well, and calls for reform were widespread. Peasants increasingly felt that they should have more respect and a say in the governing of their lives and land. The result was rebellions against the authorities. Generally these were short-lived, but some had limited success. In the Alps, a peasant rebellion began in the 14th century and eventually led to the independent state of Switzerland.

Many peasant movements called for constitutional reform. Some asked for an increase in the emperor's power, hoping to unify German territory under a common set of laws. Small numbers of nobles and clerics also called for reform. The *Bandschuh* movement (named after the peasant's low, ankle-laced shoe) mobilized tens of thousands of peasants from Swabia and Franconia into revolutionary armies in the Peasant Rebellion of 1525. But they were defeated and harshly punished, without gaining any changes in their social or political status. It is no accident that in the next century most early German immigrants came from these parts of Germany. Nuremberg observer Sebastian Franck commented in 1534 that the peasant was simply "everybody's foot-rag."

As the 16th century wore on, the Hapsburgs, through successive elections, developed a firm claim on the imperial throne. The German princes still sharply limited the emperor's power, especially in the area of raising taxes or armies. But efforts continued to give Germany some consistent, unified legal system.

East Prussia

In the many states of Germany, rulers varied from the most forward-looking to the worst tyrants. The old feudal systems that had bound farmers and other laborers to lords broke down earliest in the Rhineland. They lasted longest in the "colonial" lands to the east, especially in East Prussia. There an "upper layer" of German nobles and merchants ruled over the peasants, many of them Slavs.

Powerful landowners called *Junkers*, many of them descended from medieval knights, decided all economic, social, and political issues relating to people of the eastern marshlands. These Junkers were largely a law unto themselves. Only in the 17th century did the Elector of Brandenburg begin to impose a more unified rule over the eastern territories from the central city of Berlin.

Life in the eastern lands was harsh, for both Germans and Slavs. Peasants worked poor land with rather primitive tools. The East Prussians, under the influence of groups like the Teutonic Knights, developed a strong emphasis on military discipline. They stressed the rights of the state over the rights of the individual. In the late 19th and early 20th centuries, these ideas would come to dominate Germany as a whole, including the freer, more tolerant, and somewhat more advanced western German lands. That would help pave the way for two dreadful world wars.

The Reformation

In Germany, politics and religion had long been intertwined. Large pieces of German territory were under the direct rule of church officials. These officials, and much of the church in Italy as well, had become more secular. That is, they were less religious and more concerned with political and monetary affairs. In Northern Europe, this clashed with a strong popular desire for *more*—not less—religion in daily life.

As a result, many Germans, from peasants to scholars, began calling for a reform of the church. They wanted to disentangle religious officials from concerns with politics and money. In 15th-century France, the pope's control over the government had been reduced. Germany sought similar freedom at several diets (congresses), such as those at Augsburg in 1518 and Worms in 1521. These were aimed at curbing the abuses of clerical officials in financial matters. Perhaps most grievous of these was the widespread "sale" of indulgences—release from earthly punishment for a person's sins—to make the church richer.

It was the sale and abuse of indulgences—sometimes called "easy conscience tickets"—that disturbed a young Wittenberg monk named Martin Luther. On October 31, 1517, Luther nailed to the door of the Wittenberg church 95 theses—questions about this corrupt sale of indulgences. He could not know that he was sparking a religious revolution.

Calls for church reform were not new. And Luther was not the first to suggest that faith, not the church, was the source of salvation. Others, too, had felt that Christians should rely on their own consciences, not the church, in interpreting the Bible and judging their actions. Some Northern Europeans who felt that way had established *lay* (non-church) groups for worship.

The Netherlands group called the Brothers of the Common Life had been formed as early as 1400. Aiming to live an ideal Christian life, these

The founder of Protestantism, Martin Luther (center), shown with his family on Christmas Eve in 1538, is credited with beginning the practice of having a decorated tree in the house during the Christmas holidays. (Engraving by J. Bannister, after Schwerdgeburth, Sartain's Magazine, Library of Congress)

Brothers pooled their worldly goods, lived together in branch houses, and elected their own leader, called a *rector*. They were much like some of the medieval religious orders, but they remained laymen and existed outside of and independent of the Catholic Church—though they did not oppose it. These Brothers of the Common Life spread not only in the Netherlands but also into the Rhineland and elsewhere in Germany. Through their many schools, they reached a wide population and provided part of the basis for the religious transformation to come.

Luther did not, apparently, intend a revolution. At first he called for the church to reform itself. But the pope refused to act and, instead, expelled Luther from the church. The emperor, Charles V, banned Luther from the Holy Roman Empire. But several of the northern German princes, notably the Elector of Saxony, protected him, defying both pope and emperor.

Luther, in his refuge, was translating the Bible into German. Meanwhile his supporters grew more and more active in his defense. Often political and financial motives mixed with religious ones. Many states and free cities, seeing a chance to free themselves from church control, proclaimed themselves "Lutherans." In these new Lutheran states, former church lands became royal lands. Like the emperor, most bishops and archbishops owed their positions to the pope, and so remained loyal to the church. But even some church states turned Lutheran. East Prussia, still under the Order of the Teutonic Knights, became Lutheran in 1525, when its elected leader, Albert of Brandenburg, adopted the reformed religion.

Peasants, too, joined in. The Peasant Rebellion of 1525 was sparked, in part, by the revolutionary possibilities opened up by Luther's call for reform. Luther himself had little sympathy for the actions of this peasant army, and called for it to be ruthlessly put down—which it was.

The Catholic Holy Roman Emperor, Charles V, was involved in a desperate war with the Moslem Turks, who had driven deep into Europe and laid siege to Vienna in 1529. The emperor urged the Catholic Church to come to some agreement with the *Protestants*, as Luther's supporters came to be called. But in vain. After years of argument and delay, the Protestant and Catholic states of Germany went to war in 1546.

The religious civil war ended in 1555 with the Peace of Augsburg, which gave states the freedom to choose their own religion. This set the principle of *cuius regio eius religio*—that is, the religion of the ruler is the religion of the state. Most of the northern German states chose to be Lutheran. Most of the southern states were Catholic, especially in the Rhine Valley and in the lands directly ruled by the Hapsburgs, including the Netherlands.

The result was that Germany's population was roughly divided between Catholic and Protestant states. This was in sharp contrast to other countries, such as in Scandinavia and England, which became clearly Protestant states, though still containing some Catholic citizens. A so-called Counter-Reformation did belatedly produce some reforms in the Catholic Church, but that did little to change the religious balance of power in Germany.

Calvinism

Another 16th-century religious reformer had a powerful effect on the German people: John Calvin, a Frenchman born Jean Cauvin. Originally a follower of Luther, Calvin differed from his leader in two main ways. He believed in *predestination*—that is, that salvation comes through divine grace alone, not through any human actions. He also believed that the people should be ruled by the church, not by the state, and urged to live carefully controlled, disciplined, saintly lives.

Word of Calvin's teachings spread throughout Northern Europe. He was brought to Geneva, Switzerland, to establish his strict rule. Religious reformers from all over Europe came to see this new "ideal" religious community in action. Many went home and established Calvinist communities there.

Since Calvinists thought the church should rule, they were not welcomed by the governments of either Lutheran or Catholic states. They often faced discrimination, whether they were in the lowlands of Belgium or Holland, in France (where they were called Huguenots), in Scotland (where, following John Knox, they were called Presbyterians), or elsewhere. In some of the German states, however, Calvinism became a third acceptable religion for princes to choose. Some Calvinists from other countries therefore found refuge in German states. Many of these refugees would later go to America.

Religious Wars

There was good reason to seek refuge, for the next hundred years, from the mid-16th to the mid-17th century, saw Europe involved in a series of bloody wars, mixing religion, politics, and money. The worst of these was the Thirty Years' War between 1618 and 1648.

By the early 17th century "Germany" was more of a patchwork than before, with over 300 states, large and small. Where once the Germans had led an international trading network, now the Lutherans dealt almost exclusively with the small Protestant world. The Dutch, at the mouth of the Rhine, had largely taken over the international trade, and the cultural benefits that came with it. Northern German universities, too, were isolated. The general population was poorly educated and superstitious, much given to witch-burning. More and more people were becoming Calvinists, and demanding equality with the Lutherans in Germany.

Against this background, civil war erupted between the Catholic and Protestant states of Germany. With the tangle of political alliances typical of Europe, this placed Germany at the center of an international war, in which the French were fighting the Hapsburg emperors, the Spanish were fighting the Dutch, and everyone from the Danes and Swedes to the Bohemians and Transylvanians became involved. The three decades of fighting ended for the Germans only with the Peace of Westphalia in 1648.

In the end the treaty affirmed that each German state's ruler could choose the people's religion. The treaty also made Calvinism one of the three acceptable religions, along with Lutheranism and Catholicism. Protestant states were also allowed to hold on to former Catholic Church lands. Bavaria finally gained a vote in Germany's Electoral College, bringing to eight the number of electors selecting the Holy Roman Emperor. Later Hanover gained a vote as well.

The long-rebellious Swiss cantons, including part of old Swabia, finally became independent of the Holy Roman Empire. So did the Netherlands, at that time called the United Provinces. The Dutch held the important lands at the mouth of the Rhine River. France gained the Alsace.

After Westphalia

Under the Treaty of Westphalia, the state of Brandenburg gained territory from surrounding states. Its rulers, the Hohenzollern family, grew increasingly powerful. Later, in the 19th century, Germany would finally be unified as an empire, separate from the Holy Roman Empire. Then the Hohenzollerns would become the country's emperors, being crowned at Königsberg and ruling from Berlin.

Despite great losses, the Hapsburg emperor still ruled large territories. Many states in the empire were directly ruled by their princes. The Hapsburgs themselves were princes in some states, notably Austria and Hungary. Later, when the German Empire was created, the remnants left to the emperor would be known as the Austro-Hungarian Empire.

The emperor's power was severely restricted at Westphalia. He was barred from making any new laws regarding the states, raising taxes, or recruiting an army. War or peace in the empire could only be declared by a meeting of the princes of the 300 or so now-independent states, assembled in a congress called the *Reichstag*.

The Jews of Europe were also caught up in this terrible series of religious wars. Some Jews earlier expelled from other countries had found refuge in the 15th and 16th centuries in the Netherlands, Denmark, and some of the Italian city-states. Then in the mid-17th century, Poles and Russians began large-scale massacres, killing tens of thousands of Jews in Eastern Europe. From then on, large numbers of Jews found refuge in German cities and states—though they still faced much prejudice and heavy restrictions there.

After the Peace of Westphalia, Germany's states became fully independent. Critics of monarchy applauded this freedom, but the immediate practical result was chaos in Germany. This is partly because German lands had been devastated by the war. Armies passing across the face of the land had looted and pillaged. People had been tortured and killed, their homes and livelihoods destroyed. The survivors faced disease and starvation. Some parts of Germany lost as many as one-third to two-thirds of their people in the Thirty Years' War. Some towns were completely depopulated and left to the wolves. Some areas were not resettled for over a century.

In the wake of these terrible times, the first Germans began to migrate to America.

3

Golden Promises

Like most immigrants throughout history, many early Germans traveled in search of work. Some traveled seasonally down the Rhine to pick up extra work during the Dutch harvest season. Some would stay, finding employment in the prosperous Dutch ports. In the 17th century, when ships from Northern Europe began to cross the ocean to America, small numbers of Germans went along, among them farm laborers, skilled artisans, and soldiers. With their skills and their capacity for hard work, they generally prospered in the new land.

In the next few centuries, Germans would go to America for many reasons and under varying conditions. One of the most important reasons for emigration—leaving their homeland—would continue to be the desire for work and the chance to make a better living. The pattern of traveling down the Rhine to Holland made emigration that much easier for people who lived in western Germany, in the states near the river.

Religious Freedom

The earliest groups of German immigrants came to America not in search of work but largely for religious reasons. The 1648 Treaty of Westphalia had recognized three religions in the German states: Lutheran, Roman Catholic, and Calvinist, also called Reformed. But many other smaller religious groups called *sects* existed, too. These sects differed from each other, but generally stressed inner faith, rather than church organization. Many had no churches, preferring to worship in private homes. Many had no specially trained ministers, believing that anyone could be a spiritual leader.

Many of these sectarians were inspired by John Huss, a Bohemian martyred in the early 15th century, a century before Luther. Persecuted in Europe since that time, some of Huss' followers—often called Anabaptists—had sought refuge in Switzerland, the Palatinate, and the Netherlands before they found haven in America. Sometimes whole congregations of these religious dissidents would flee together.

The Mennonites, discriminated against in their homeland, took their name from their early leader, Menno Simons.
(Library of Congress)

One group of Anabaptists was led by Menno Simons; these were the Mennonites. A smaller group, split off from the Mennonites, was led by Jakob Amman; these were the Amish. Another group was the German Baptists Brethren, generally called Dunkers or Dunkards, after their practice of dunking the whole person, rather than sprinkling water, during baptism. The Hutterites were follower of Jakob Hutter, a religious leader from Moravia (in modern Czechoslovakia).

The Moravians, also called the United Brethren, hoped to bring together all Protestant groups, and emphasized their common beliefs, rather than their differences. The Schwenkfelders, from the region of Silesia, had been persistently persecuted since Luther's time.

To the established churches and governments, these sectarians were unbelievers. At best, they lived in an atmosphere of disapproval. At worst, their worship was considered illegal and they were expelled from their homes. Some, notably the Schwenkfelders and Moravians, found refuge in Saxony on the estate of Count Nikolaus von Zinzendorf. This extraordinary man aided many of Europe's religious refugees and helped bring them to America. The Moravians were even sometimes called the Herrnhuter, after Zinzendorf's estate, Herrnhut, meaning "The Lord's Watch."

Many sectarians looked to America as a land of religious tolerance, where they could form separate communities away from the corruption of the Old World. As a result they were very open to the message of William Penn and the Quakers, English sectarians who also stressed the individual's inner faith.

Early Quaker missionaries had come to Germany in the 1650s. When Penn himself arrived in Germany in 1671, he found some small Quaker communities, such as that in the Palatine city of Kriegsheim. Penn himself made many converts in regions like the Palatinate and Holstein, and in cities like Lübeck, Hamburg, and Krefeld. On his second trip to Germany in 1677, Penn had even more success, converting many influential people in the Rhineland and especially in Frankfurt-am-Main (on the Main River).

Many other sectarians were also attracted by Penn's vision of a new community along the Delaware River. A group of sectarians from Frankfurt-am-Main formed a company and in 1683 bought acreage in Pennsylvania, intending to form a religious community. A highly educated young lawyer named Francis (in Germany, Franz) Daniel Pastorius had this reaction to the Frankfurt Company's plans: "This begat a desire in my soul to continue in their society and with them to lead a quiet, godly, and honest life in a howling wilderness."

None of the shareholders actually came to America, but Pastorius did. Acting as agent for the company, he led a party of 13 families, Mennonites and Quakers, from Krefeld. They were the first of many.

Germans of the accepted religions came to America, too. German rulers who forced their religion on their state's population drove many into exile. In 1731, for example over 30,000 Protestants were exiled from Salzburg, Austria, by the Catholic archbishop. Though sectarians predominated in the early German immigration to America, Germans of the Lutheran and Reformed churches later would come to far outnumber the sectarians in the new land.

Hard Times

Many early German immigrants were also drawn to America by a strong desire to live in a country free of constant warfare. The Thirty Years' War had devastated Germany, especially the Palatinate and the surrounding districts of southwest Germany. Even after the war's end, French Catholic armies continued to march back and forth through the Rhineland for decades. In May of 1707, for example, a French army marched into southwestern Germany—to the Palatinate, Württemberg,

Baden, and Swabia—and stayed for four months. An English observer noted that the French marshal had "not only maintained a great army in [the area] all the year, but by contributions, sent money into France to help the King's other affairs."

Like agricultural people everywhere, Germans were also subject to natural disasters. The winter of 1708-1709 was an especially bitter one. Writers surely exaggerated when they reported that in January wine froze into solid blocks and birds fell dead in mid-flight. But it *was* one of the harshest winters on record. Many fruit trees and vines were killed by the deep frost and heavy snow. Over half of those who left Germany in the following few years were farm and vineyard workers. Over the next two centuries, periodic crop failures would send waves of emigrants from Germany.

Many Germans came to America because they had outgrown the small amount of land they occupied. This was especially important in the southwest German provinces because there family farms—however small—were split up among all the children who survived their parents. So plots became ever smaller and less capable of supporting a family. In other parts of Germany the family farm was often passed on undivided to the main heir. The other children were then obliged to find other ways of supporting themselves. For some that would include going to America. Later on, as Germany's agricultural system was modernized, many people would be thrown off the land. So landless farmers and unemployed laborers would also make their way to America.

The people of the Rhineland were often heavily taxed. Many German princes wanted to live as luxuriously as France's Louis XIV. But where Louis commanded the resources of a huge country, these princes ruled only small states. One Palatine German writing in 1681 complained of the "plague of high taxes" and commented that "thousands would gladly leave the Fatherland if they had the means to do so." Taxes only grew heavier in the following decades. Then some Germans found the means to leave, by appealing to Protestant friends abroad.

The Colonies

Many early German emigrants sought aid from the Protestant English ruler, Queen Anne, stressing the hardships they had faced in the Rhine and Neckar valleys. Queen Anne *did* help some, in the early days, in the interest of her own country.

While the German emigrants wanted religious freedom, peace, land, and work, the British wanted settlers in their new American colonies. Many of the colonies were run mainly as businesses. Settlers were needed to work the land and produce profits, which would then be shared by the business owners and the British crown.

The British desire for settlers was so strong that they even offered immigrants citizenship, under the Naturalization Act of 1671. A broader act in 1680 aimed to provide "all possible encouragement . . . to persons of different nations to transport themselves hither with their families and stocks, to settle, plant or reside . . ."

Pennsylvania and Carolina were particularly eager for settlers in the early 18th century. Agents for these colonies wrote pamphlets and books telling of the wonderful new land. These enormously attractive writings were distributed up and down the Rhine Valley.

One book even hinted at royal support by including a picture of Britain's Queen Anne. Because its title was lettered in gold, this widely read work came to be called "The Golden Book." One 1709 emigrant, Ulrich Simmendinger, wrote that he and many others left Germany because they had received "golden promises"—of royal support—from the British. Few German emigrants actually received aid, but others kept leaving on the strength of hope.

America Letters

Even without hope of aid, Germans were attracted by what they read and heard about America. Many German settlers wrote books and reports about their life in the new land. In 1700, Francis Pastorius published a description of Pennsylvania, which was widely circulated in Germany. Later editions of the work, with additions from other authors, were used to advertise the settlement among the German population.

Following the standard immigrant pattern, early German settlers in America also wrote letters to family and friends back home. These were the so-called "America letters," through which many people learned of the new land. The promise of peace, religious freedom, and economic opportunity attracted increasing numbers of emigrants through the 18th century. Many, quite naturally, headed for German settlements in America, and then fanned out from there—soon writing their own America letters back home. Throughout this early period, most immigrants traveled in large groups, generally made up of families, with some young single men and women.

Revolutionary Times

A different type of immigrant came during the American Revolution. Then some young German men, excited about the possibilities of a new, independent democracy, crossed the ocean to fight either in the American army directly or in the allied French army. How many came is not at all clear.

Many more Germans—some 30,000—were brought over to fight on the British side as mercenaries. These were soldiers in German armies, who had been "rented" to the British for cash. Though drawn from several other states as well as Hesse, in America German soldiers all were called "Hessians."

But events in Europe soon closed off emigration from Germany. In the years after the French Revolution of 1789, the rise of Napoleon engulfed Europe in a series of wars. Even the distant Americas were involved. Many German states, not wanting to lose potential soldiers and farmers, barred emigration. The French, under Napoleon, took the main Rhine seaports and restricted travel. Pirates and privateers ruled the ocean waves. With battles raging on land and sea, not many immigrants found their way out of Europe to the United States. In the whole of 1812 only one immigrant ship arrived from Germany.

The Auswanderer

But the pressure to leave continued to grow. People in the German heartland were bone-weary of the never-ending wars. They longed for peace and freedom, for the day when armies would cease running over their land. That day finally came in 1815, with the end of the Age of Napoleon.

But prosperity did not follow. The mid-1810s saw a series of poor harvests. The worst of these by far occurred in the year 1816. Cold, rainy, and violent weather persisted throughout the year. The harvest was almost nonexistent and, because of the wars, there were no real reserves against famine. The result was starvation on every side. People ate whatever they could find—roots, grasses, and mosses. A German medical professor even wrote a book about how to prepare bread out of sawdust. Even where there was food to buy, few could pay for it, for most had no work. Laborers, skilled and unskilled, could find no paying jobs.

The result was a massive, desperate migration called the *Auswanderung*—the "wandering out." Beginning in late 1816, tens of thousands of Germans left their homes. Some went east, especially into Russia; some of those—later in the century—would reenter our story as Russian-German immigrants to North America. Many went to South America. But many others were drawn to America. Along with tales of success and freedom, some American friends and relatives even sent prepaid tickets so they could leave Germany.

As some of these new immigrants began to spread out in America—into Ohio, Kentucky, Missouri, and other farming lands—they, too, wrote America letters and books. One of the most influential of these books was written by a well-educated German immigrant, Gottfried Duden, who had bought 275 acres of land near where the Missouri River joins the Mississippi. Published in Germany in 1829, Duden's description of the beautiful land, its democracy, and its opportunities attracted many immigrants. European visitors also wrote of their travels in America. Frenchman Alexis de Tocqueville's *Democracy in America*, first published in 1835, was translated into German and widely read. His views of American democracy were eagerly debated, especially by liberal Germans who were attempting to bring about democractic reform in Germany.

Highly trained German chemists and pharmacists for centuries had fine, heavily regulated shops like this one in 17th-century Frankfurt, while in 19th-century America, people with no training at all could open up a shop selling medicines.
(Author's archives)

The books about America attracted a new type of immigrant to America. Many highly skilled, well-educated professionals—doctors, lawyers, professors, teachers, scientists, industrialists, traders, and the like, sometimes wealthy and even aristocratic Germans—joined the emigration. These immigrants were also drawn from different parts of Germany, especially the north around Westphalia and Hanover.

But these new immigrants were far outnumbered by farm families hoping to take advantage of cheap land to be found on the frontier. With successive crop failures, their numbers swelled. The worst failure was the potato blight of the 1840s. As in Ireland, the potato had become a staple in the diet of many German farm families. The blight caused the potatoes to rot in the fields and storehouses, leaving thousands of people to starve. These were not necessarily the people who emigrated, for money was needed to travel all the way to America. But the whole economic and social fabric of the German states was badly disrupted by the potato blight and the resulting famine. The result was a steeply rising wave of German immigrants to America.

All over Germany, emigration assocations—some with their own newspapers—were formed to advise emigrants. Some, such as the Association for the Protection of German Immigrants in Texas, had ties with particular parts of the United States. They helped potential emigrants plan for their journey.

A small number of emigrants in this period left Germany for religious reasons. In Prussia, the rulers had merged the Lutheran and Reformed churches in 1817. Some "Old Lutherans," who opposed the merger, emigrated to the United States. But from the early 19th century, most emigrants would leave Germany for economic, social, or political reasons.

The Liberals

Political reasons were the leading cause of emigration for many Germans in the mid-19th century. Intellectuals and reformers had long dreamed of a united, democratic Germany. Scholars, students, and liberals of varied backgrounds had joined together in various reform organizations. Among these were *Turner* societies, which combined beliefs in physical fitness and democratic reform.

Many German princes had promised that, once Napoleon was defeated, they would allow more freedom and liberty to German citizens. But they quickly broke their promises. Under the Austrian Prince Metternich, a period of sharp repression and censorship followed. Even before 1820, some liberal leaders were jailed, and many others left the country for America.

The problems of Germany were not simple. At the end of the Napoleonic Wars, the German states had joined in a Germanic Confederation, the two most powerful states being Prussia and Austria. Representatives of all the states met in a congress called a diet in Frankfurt. Many Germans wanted a unified state for all the German people. But the empire, especially Austria and Hungary, included large numbers of non-German peoples.

Without unification, little reform would take place. Most political power was still firmly in the hands of the rich and the aristocrats. Workers, farmers, and people of the middle classes had nothing like equal representation. Police spies were everywhere.

A fragmented Germany also meant that trade and industry had little chance to grow freely. Each state imposed its own taxes and fees, and effectively strangled modernization. Old ways of farming also hampered production.

Liberal organizations continued to work for reform. Occasional uprisings, such as that in Frankfurt in 1833, were sharply put down. Each one sent new liberal immigrants to America. Many liberals stayed, however, and continued to work for reform in Germany.

During the revolutions of 1848 in Germany, liberals—many of them students—fought government troops in the streets, as here in Berlin.
(Library of Congress)

In the year of 1848, with revolutions sweeping many nations in Europe, the liberals were successful for a time in Germany. They elected an 800-member popular assembly, the Frankfurt Parliament, to shape a new, unified, democratic German state. Unfortunately, the delegates were divided on many issues, especially this crucial question: Should the new state be a constitutional monarchy, as in Great Britain or Scandinavia, or an independent republic, as in the United States?

In the end, the delegates' inability to decide among themselves doomed reform efforts. The Frankfurt Parliament collapsed, dashing hopes for liberal reform. Prussia took over the process of uniting Germany, without Austria. After that, thousands of liberal reformers left Germany for America. These so-called "Forty-Eighters" would have an emormous impact on the shaping of modern America.

The Main Wave

But the Forty-Eighters were far outnumbered by the truly massive wave of German emigrants that began in the 1850s. Between 1852 and 1854 alone, over 500,000 people left Germany, many of them for America.

Immigration by families slowed somewhat during the years of the Civil War, though many single young men came to fight in the war and be rewarded after it with citizenship and free land in the West. Then at war's end, immigration boomed again. Between 1866 and 1873 German immigrants came to America at the rate of about 130,000 a year. An economic depression in America slowed immigration somewhat after 1873, but the numbers soared again in the 1880s, reaching a peak of some 250,000 in the single year of 1882. Only then did the numbers decline, and the great wave of German emigration finally begin to ebb.

Even so, the number of German immigrants in this wave was astonishing. Between the end of the Napoleonic Wars and the beginning of World War I, over five million immigrants came to America from the various German states. Perhaps as many as one or two million more Germans came from other countries, especially Switzerland, Russia, and Austria.

The spurs for this massive migration were the same as those of the earlier Auswanderers. The economic hardship of a fragmented Germany often at war continued. So did the pressure of too many people and too little land. Heavy taxation, required military service, and political oppression also pushed people to leave home.

But the attractions of America in this period were perhaps even more important. Through letters and reports from the early Auswanderers, word of America had spread ever more widely in Germany, especially word of cheap or free land in the West. Better and cheaper transportation—railroad and steamships—meant that many more of them could take advantage of what America had to offer. Certainly when America was in an economic slump, as in the 1870s, immigration slowed. When America boomed, it picked up again.

Russian Germans

Added to this main wave of the Auswanderers were many Germans from Russia. Between 1763 and the 1820s, tens of thousands of Germans had been recruited to live in Russia. They were settled in mostly independent, German-speaking colonies along the Volga River and, after 1804, north of the Black Sea. There they were given land and money for tools, were exempted from military service, and granted freedom of religion.

The German settlers came from much the same regions of southwest Germany as the early German-American settlers. And they had the same mix of religions—mostly Lutheran and Reformed, some Catholics, and some sectarian groups, including Mennonites and Hutterites. The colonies had succeeded, and even founded some offshoot colonies elsewhere in Russia, still keeping their separate German culture. By the 1870s, there were hundreds of thousands of these Russian-Germans, perhaps over a million.

Then in 1871, Czar Alexander II revoked the guarantees given by the previous rulers. Young Russian-German men were required to serve in the Russian army and the colonies' separateness came under serious attack. Starting in the following year, scouting parties and then large groups of Russian-German settlers began migrating to the United States, mostly to the upper Midwest, and also into western Canada. In all, 200,000 or more came to North America.

Modern Times

The pattern of heavy German emigration would alter only as Germany itself began to change. In 1871 the German states united. They went to war with France and won. The Franco-Prussian War, as it was called, brought the Alsace-Lorraine into German hands. To Germans the fruits of unity could not have been sweeter. After the war, the united states proclaimed themselves the German Empire. Chancellor Otto von Bismarck was the chief architect of German unity. The German Empire's ruler was called the Kaiser, the German form of the old Roman title of Caesar. There were new laws, designed to better the life of the population. Economic and social pressures eased somewhat. Germany's own industrialization was, by then, in full swing and providing more jobs at home.

At the same time, America was facing periodic economic crises, especially in 1893. German immigration gradually slowed. By the 1890s, the American frontier was mostly gone—and with it the cheap land. Then, too, German skills were no longer so necessary or prized. America's new heavy industry relied less on skilled artisans than on large numbers of semi-skilled factory workers.

But if changes under the German Empire slowed emigration from among the general population, it spurred some groups to leave. German Catholics and Jews faced increasing social and economic discrimination. Socialists, too, were subject to restrictive laws after 1878. Many young men wanted to avoid military service in the new imperial army. These groups made up a somewhat larger proportion of the emigration than before.

Where families had traditionally made up two-thirds or more of the immigrant population, from the 1890s, single workers dominated. Many of these planned to make money working in America's high-paying industries, and then return home. Later some of them did just that.

Emigration slowed sharply during World War I. Young men were wanted as soldiers in Germany. And even before the United States entered the war in 1917, growing anti-German feeling in America discouraged much German immigration.

Though the war left Germany in economic ruin, one sign of hope was the founding of a German democracy—the Weimar Republic. But runaway inflation and depression doomed the democracy and sent thousands of new immigrants to America. And Germans turned to a new leader, an Austrian-born German named Adolf Hitler.

Hitler Years

Hitler and the Nazi party gave many of the German people hope of economic revival in the early 1930s. With America in Depression, some

German immigrants even went back home to try to rebuild Germany. For the only time in history, more people left America for Germany than the reverse. (This was partly because Americans had, starting in the 1920s, imposed annual limits on the number of immigrants allowed in from each country.)

But Hitler's rule quickly changed the atmosphere in Germany. The country came to be dominated by some of the worst tendencies in its history—unchecked militarism, glorification of the supposedly pure "Aryan" race, hatred of other peoples, especially Jews, and the wholesale killing of enemies. Some people could see that Germany was becoming a dangerous place for them and, by the mid-1930s, were trying to leave Germany. Most were Jews and people whose politics disagreed sharply with those of the Nazis. Many others, not directly in danger, left on principle, revolted by the anti-democratic turn Germany had taken or fearful that war would once again engulf Europe.

Like the Forty-Eighters of a century before, many of the refugees from Hitler's Germany to America were highly educated, immensely talented people. And like those earlier immigrants, they would have a powerful impact on their new homeland.

Unfortunately, because of immigration quotas, many of the religious and political refugees from Hitler's Germany were turned away from

In personal writings and in massive public rallies, like this one at Nuremberg, Adolf Hitler (third from right) made clear his terrible vision of a "new Germany," based on hatred and violence.

America. Some found refuge in other countries, but many others had to return to Europe. Later, during World War II, they—along with others who had not believed they were in danger—were caught up in the terrible killing organization of the Nazis, in which millions of people died.

Under Hitler, Germany once again expanded. The Nazi "argument" was that Germans needed "elbow room," and that many neighboring lands were "naturally" German territory, because Germans lived there. Using this argument, the Germans annexed Czechoslovakia and Austria, with only weak protest from other European countries. Then they divided up Poland with the Russians. (Germany had held much of Poland from the late 18th century to World War I, and many Germans were settled there.) That finally provoked World War II, in which most Western European countries, and later the United States and Russia, fought the Germans and Italians in Europe. After astonishing early successes, Hitler's Germans overextended themselves and were finally defeated in 1945.

After the War

At the end of the war Germany's borders were altered dramatically. A new independent Polish state was formed, this one farther west than the pre-war one, and including territory from the former German Empire, notably ore-rich Silesia. The Alsace, which Germany had lost in World War I and then taken back, went to France once again. Austria and Czechoslovakia regained their independence. The remaining shell of Germany was split into two countries: West Germany, centered on the Rhineland, and East Germany, centered around Berlin, which became an "international city" governed by the victors. The Eastern European countries, except Austria, came under the domination of Communist Russia. Germany itself was blasted beyond recognition in many areas.

German immigrants were quite different, too, in the years after World War II. Many of them were displaced persons or refugees, especially Jews and people from East Germany. Many others were wives and families of American servicemen stationed in Germany after the war—as continues to be true.

Today East Germany is still under Russian control, divided from West Germany by a physical barrier, and Berlin is a divided city. East Germans cannot emigrate freely. West Germans can, but few do so—if only because West Germany has a very high standard of living. Those who do immigrate are often highly educated individuals.

4

The Journey

[Immigrants] were commonly treated with the least possible attention, with the utmost disregard of decency and humanity. With rare exceptions they were robbed and plundered from the day of their departure to the moment of their arrival at their new homes, by almost everyone with whom they came in contact . . . There seemed to be a secret league, a tacit conspiracy, on the part of all parties dealing with immigrants to fleece and pluck them without mercy, and then send them from hand to hand as long as anything could be made of them . . .

Friedrich Kapp, Geschichte der Deutschen im Staate New York, 1867, *reporting to an immigrant aid society*

The first group of German emigrants made their way to America with the help of friends. Francis Daniel Pastorius, leader of the Krefeld party and agent for the Frankfurt Company, made the arrangements through William Penn's agent. Pastorius himself, accompanied by a few men and women servants, sailed on ahead to America, to prepare the way for the new community.

Six weeks later, the Krefeld party followed. Like many later emigrants, the Krefeld party journeyed down the Rhine River into the Netherlands, to the major port of Rotterdam. Their ship, the *Concord*—for Germans much like the Pilgrims' *Mayflower*—was a solid vessel, which had seen service in the West Indies. Unlike the ships in which many later immigrants would cross the Atlantic, it was relatively spacious. After crossing the English Channel to Gravesend, England, the ship left for America on July 24, 1683, arriving in Philadelphia on October 6, 1683. The fare was 5 pounds per person, 2 1/2 pounds for children under 12. They had a rather safe and uneventful journey, but other emigrants to follow would have more difficulty.

Leaving Home

For early emigrants, leaving home was neither simple nor easy. In rural Germany, many peasants were still bound, sometimes by law, to the land. The German states were not anxious to lose their citizens—potential farmers, soldiers, and workers—so local governments often barred emigration outside German territory.

People who wished to depart often had to get a dozen or more permits and other papers from the state. They must have paid all taxes and performed any required military service. Many of them were obliged to give up their citizenship on leaving.

For those emigrants with enough money, boatmen were eager to supply passage down the Rhine. Most other emigrants—and everyone during the winter, when ice clogged the channel—followed roads alongside the river. On their way down the Rhine, by road or river, travelers had to pay tolls at as many as 40 collection points, before they finally reached the sea. Gottlieb Mittelberger—who left probably the finest record of an emigrant journey from this period—explained his trip from Germany to America in 1750:

This is the Rhineland, heavily farmed hills and valleys, dotted with castles, all overlooking the Rhine River, the German emigrants' main route to the sea.
(Library of Congress)

This [whole] journey lasts from the beginning of May until the end of October, that is, a whole six months, and involves such hardships that it is really impossible for any description to do justice to them . . . At each [customs house] all the ships must be examined, and these examinations take place at the convenience of the customs officials. Meanwhile, the ships with the people in them are held up for a long time. This involved a great deal of expense for the passengers; and it also means that the trip down the Rhine alone takes from four to six weeks.

Many feared that, if their papers were not in proper order, they might be sent back by officials—and indeed some were. On occasion whole boatloads of emigrants were stopped en route and imprisoned.

At the Ports

Those who completed the trip down the Rhine often spent their little remaining money waiting in port for the ship to America. In those early days, ships did not sail on a regular schedule, but waited until they had a full load, sometimes for as long as five or six weeks. As Mittelberger noted: "Because everything is very expensive in Holland the poor people must spend nearly all they own during this period."

After all this, relatively few emigrants still had the money to pay the fare to America. At this point many penniless emigrants—perhaps one out of four or five, by some accounts—returned home far poorer than they had left it. This was sometimes easier said than done, because many emigrants had already given up their citizenship, while others had left illegally, without papers. In practice, however, their home states generally took them back and made some effort to help them reestablish themselves. The rest of the emigrants stayed at the ports—and hoped.

The situation was wide open for fraud and exploitation. Some unscrupulous Rhine boatmen—looking for more fares—even assured emigrants that in Rotterdam or Amsterdam they would receive a gift of cash and food, free passage to America, and free land once there. Shippers and their agents sometimes made similar promises. In January 1817, a German from Swabia wrote this diary entry: "A man has been about whom the people call 'the American'; he has been persuading people to emigrate to America, where all food is said to be easy to get. Some people have left neighboring towns, too, and their villages sang hymns for them when they departed."

They might well sing hymns, for German emigrants arriving in Amsterdam trusting in these "golden promises" were bitterly disappointed. No such free passage or good fortune awaited them. Instead they found thousands of other emigrants just like themselves, crowded into the poorest sections of the ports.

In the early 18th century, some penniless German emigrants—mostly Protestants—*were* lucky enough to get aid from Dutch and British Protestants. Thousands of them ended up in refugee tent camps outside London, surviving for some months only with public and private help. Of the estimated 13,500 German emigrants camped outside London in 1709, only about one-quarter actually reached America. Some died in the disease-ridden camps. Some went to Ireland or settled in England. Some returned home, among them over 2,200 Roman Catholics turned away by the British Protestants. British Protestants could not aid the thousands who followed, however. Many would-be emigrants had neither the personal funds nor the help to leave mainland Europe.

Redemption

Penniless emigrants did have a choice, though—a bitter one. At the mouth of the Rhine, in Netherlands ports such as Rotterdam and Amsterdam, they found many cargo ships that had brought goods from America. The ships' captains were delighted at the prospect of human "cargo" to fill their holds on the voyage back across the Atlantic. Seeing the possibility of profit, Dutch and British shippers developed a system called *redemption.*

Emigrants were shipped across the Atlantic without paying any fare. In return, they had to sign a contract agreeing to repay or *redeem* the "loan" of the passage money within a specified time after their arrival in America—say, within two weeks. If they could not redeem the loan in time—and most could not—the captain would sell the contract to the highest bidder. The unfortunate immigrant would then be obliged to work as a virtual slave to the contract holder for a number of years.

Such immigrants were called *redemptioners, bond servants,* or *indentured servants.* As many as one-half to two-thirds of the German immigrants in colonial times entered America as redemptioners. Many English immigrants came as indentured servants, too, but the time they were to serve was generally specified before they left Europe. That for German redemptioners was not. The terms of service generally ranged from four to eight years, though children served until age 21.

Redemptioners were not slaves, since their term of service was limited by contract. But they had little more freedom than slaves. Immigrant families were sometimes sold into service for different people, many miles apart, and so were separated in the new land. At first, the people who held these contracts were usually earlier British settlers. Later many redemptioners found themselves working for prosperous German colonists.

The German-American community was sharply divided about the practice of redemption. Wealthy Germans, such as New York's Jacob Leisler, sometimes paid the fare for penniless families on arrival. There were far too many poor newcomers, however, for such benefactors to be able to help. As early as 1764, Philadelphia's German-American Society—the first non-religious society Germans founded in America—was established to protest the redemption trade. Branches of the same movement were founded elsewhere, in Charleston in 1766, in Baltimore in 1783, and in New York City in 1784.

Shippers profited handsomely from these redemption arrangements. They even sent agents called *newlanders* into Germany to encourage more people to emigrate. Gottlieb Mittelberger protested bitterly against those "man-stealing" agents, who "steal German people under all sorts of fine pretexts, and deliver them into the hands of the great Dutch traffickers in human souls." Even some Germans who left home prosperous and with plenty of money could become redemptioners after losing money to outright thieves or trusting it to newlanders who promised to "take care of it" and then disappeared.

The plight of redemptioners in America was very sad. Mittelberger later wrote a book about his experience because he had taken "a solemn oath" to do so. On learning that he was returning to Germany, he reported, some redemptioners:

> . . . begged me with tears and uplifted hands, and even in the name of God, to publicize their misery and sorrow in Germany. So that not only the common people but even princes and lords might be able to hear about what happened to them; and so that innocent souls would no longer leave their native country, persuaded to do so by Newlanders, and dragged by them into a similar kind of slavery.

Word of the hard life faced by redemptioners did gradually filter back into Germany, through America letters and reports like Mittelberger's. Even so, the trade in contracts of poor German immigrants survived until 1819.

Early Voyages

Throughout this time, the German emigrants' main route to America lay down the Rhine Valley to the Dutch ports of Rotterdam or Amsterdam. From there, they often traveled to England, where they spent days or perhaps weeks, until the ship was full. Only then did the ship leave for America. Early German immigrant ships generally headed for the port of Philadelphia, though many went to other ports as well, including New York, Baltimore, and Charleston.

These small sailing ships were cramped and desperately crowded, carrying as many as 400 to 600 passengers. As Mittelberger put it, people were packed "as closely as herring," with each person's sleeping space barely two feet by six feet. Food and fresh water were poor and in short supply. Mittelberger noted:

Sailing ships like this one at Philadelphia's Arch Street Ferry brought immigrants from Europe to all the main East Coast ports. (Engraving by William Birch & Son, from *The City of Philadelphia . . . .* 1800, Library of Congress)

During the journey the ship is full of pitiful signs of distress—smells, fumes, horrors, vomiting, various kinds of sea sickness, fever, dysentery, headaches, heat, constipation, boils, scurvy, cancer, mouth-rot, and similar afflictions, all of them caused by the age and the highly-salted state of the food, especially of the meat, as well as by the very bad and filthy water, which brings about the miserable destruction and death of many. Add to all that shortage of food, hunger, thirst, frost, heat, dampness, fear, misery, vexations, and lamentation as well as other troubles. Thus, for example, there are so many lice, especially on the sick people, that they have to be scraped off the bodies. All this misery reaches its climax when in addition to everything else one must also suffer through two or three days and nights of storm, with everyone convinced that the ship with all aboard is bound to sink. In such misery all the people on board pray and cry pitifully together.

Disease spread quickly among people already weakened by weeks of traveling to ports and waiting in tent camps. The dreaded disease typhus became so common it was sometimes called "Palatine fever." Of the first main group of Palatine Germans in 1710, nearly one out of every seven people—446 out of 2,814—died during the nearly six-month-long journey out of Germany and across the Atlantic.

Mittelberger commented that few children between the ages of one and seven could survive the harsh journey. On his own journey, 32 young children died, "all of whom were finally thrown into the sea." But adults died, too. Surviving family members had to pay not only their own fares, but also the fares of those who died. Orphaned children were indentured for the cost of both the parents' fares and their own. For over 150 years, immigrants would face the same terrible conditions and experience the same terrifying loss of life on the journey.

The ships themselves were not always seaworthy. And they were traveling through some of the roughest, stormiest seas in the world, making the North Atlantic passage from Europe to America. Going west to east, the passage was relatively quick and easy. But going from east to west, ships had to buck contrary winds and currents every inch of the way. More than one ship was lost in a storm or ran aground on rocks off the North American coast, drowning all aboard, except perhaps a few who survived in a lifeboat and were lucky enough to meet with another ship that picked them up.

Even when they arrived safely in port, the journey was not over for all passengers. Those who had paid their fare were free to go ashore. But redemptioners had to remain on board the ship, under those terrible conditions, until their contracts were sold or "redeemed." The exception was that all males 15 years or older were generally taken to the local city hall to take an oath of allegiance to Great Britain before being returned to the ship. Mittelberger explained how the "commerce in human beings" worked in the mid-18th century:

> Every day Englishmen, Dutchmen, and High Germans come from Philadelphia and other places, some of them very far away, sometimes twenty or thirty or forty hours' journey, and go on board the newly arrived vessel that has brought people from Europe and offers them for sale. From among the healthy they pick out those suitable for the purposes for which they require them. Then they negotiate with them as to the length of the period for which they will go into service in order to pay off their passage, the whole amount of which they generally owe. When an agreement has been reached, adult persons by written contract bind themselves to serve for three, four, five, or six years, according to their health and age. The very young, between the ages of ten and fifteen, have to serve until they are twenty-one, however.
>
> Many parents in order to pay their fares in this way and get off the ship must barter and sell their children as if they were cattle. Since the fathers and mothers often do not know where or to what masters their children are to be sent, it frequently happens that after leaving the vessel, parents and children do not see each other for years on end, or even for the rest of their lives.

Since those who were sick did not readily find purchasers, some miserable immigrants remained at sea for two or three weeks, or even died, within sight of land. Some were eventually taken to hospital to recover, and *then* had their contracts sold to work off their fares.

Yet still they came. The numbers tell the story: In 1717, three ships carrying 363 Palatine Germans arrived in Philadelphia. (Though many came from states east of the Palatinate, all were called Palatines in America.) Between 1727, when Pennsylvania began recording immigration figures, and 1740, some 80 more shiploads of Palatines arrived. Between then and 1755, another 159 shiploads came.

Immigration ground to a halt during the later years of the French and Indian War (in Europe called the Seven Years' War). From the end of the war in 1763 to 1776, another 88 shiploads of Palatine German immigrants arrived in Philadelphia. Some, like the 40 Mennonite families who came to work in Virginia's iron mines, traveled as a congregation, complete with their pastor.

How many German immigrants had arrived in the North American colonies by the start of the Revolutionary War in 1776 is not clear. About 25,000 German immigrants arrived between 1749 and 1753; perhaps 30,000 more arrived between 1757 and 1759. Estimates of the total range from 65,000 to 100,000.

After Napoleon

During America's Revolutionary War, immigration dropped to almost nothing, except for the many German soldiers who crossed the Atlantic to fight on both sides in the war. Immigration peaked again briefly in 1782, but dropped off in just a few years. The French Revolution in 1789 and the Napoleonic Wars brought emigration from Germany nearly to a standstill for a quarter of a century. The Rhine ports, held by Napoleon, were closed to German emigration. Some immigrants, however, did continue to leave through the north German port of Bremen.

Not until the end of the Napoleonic Wars in 1815 were Germans able to travel more freely. Then the German states began to eliminate the cumbersome set of tolls and checks that had long plagued travelers at each border. Most emigrants paid their own way or were sent a prepaid ticket by someone already in America. But some German communities emptied their prisons and poorhouses and paid the occupants to go to America—though sometimes the payment took them only as far as the Rhine ports. This practice would continue until the mid-19th century.

Even though the redemption system ended in 1819, some shipowners still saw profit to be made, and employed agents to attract immigrants. America's new Western states also sent agents to lure immigrants, often with fairy-tale visions of a rich life in the new land.

Through the 1830s most of the emigrants were from southwest Germany, the region around the Palatinate on the upper Rhine. Almost half of these went to South America. But after that, more emigrants began to be drawn from other parts of Germany, especially Westphalia, the lower

Rhineland, and East Prussia. And most of these went to North America, especially to the United States.

In 1847 alone, 80,000 emigrants left Germany for America. In 1854 the number peaked at over 215,000. Over 650,000 immigrants came from Germany between 1865 and 1869; and nearly 800,000 between 1880 and 1884, with 250,000 immigrants in the peak year of 1882. In this whole period, at least one quarter of the total immigrants to America were German. Only in the 1890s did the numbers begin to drop off. Even so, over 200,000 German immigrants came in the first decade of the 20th century.

New Ports

After 1815, the Rhine ports were used for a few years. But the redemption system ended, the Netherlands were in political turmoil, and these ports had a series of cholera epidemics. So German emigrants looked for new ports for their American voyage.

Many turned toward Le Havre (The Harbor). This French port had a regular trade between the American cotton country and the rising manufacturing cities of France and southern Germany. Immigrants followed the line of freight wagons to Le Havre. The rich traveled by stagecoach, sending their luggage on the slower freight wagons. But others traveled in covered wagons, like those of the American pioneers, camping by the roadside at night.

A French writer for *Chamber's Edinburgh Journal* described the scene in Bavaria in 1846. There he saw the populations of whole villages filing seaward, led by their priest or minister:

> It is a lamentable sight when you are traveling in the spring or autumn on the Strasburg road, to see the long files of carts that you meet every mile, carrying the whole property of the poor wretches, who are about to cross the Atlantic on the faith of a lying prospectus [an agent's brochure]. There they go slowly along; their miserable [carts] . . . piled with the scanty boxes containing their few effects, and on the top of all, the women and children, the sick and bedridden, and all who are too exhausted with the journey to walk. One might take it for a convoy of wounded, the relics of a battlefield, but for the rows of little white heads peeping from beneath the ragged hood.

Some headed straight for Le Havre. Others went to Paris, where they sold their horses and sailed down to the sea on the Seine River. Sometimes immigrants even dismantled their wagons, shipped them across the Atlantic, and reassembled them on the other side for their overland journey to the American West. Altogether the trip from the Rhine to the Atlantic took several weeks. Captains hired German-speaking agents—ship's brokers or "runners"—to sell space on the ship. Some worked in port, but others went out on the road to meet arriving emigrant caravans.

So many Germans headed for Le Havre that in some years the town sometimes seemed as much German as French. During the several weeks' wait for their ship, emigrants generally lodged in cheap rooming houses or camped outdoors. As in every such port, many emigrants ran out of money or were robbed. Some decided to stay or returned home. To prevent a drain on state charity, the French government began to require that each German emigrant have a ship's ticket or at least enough money to buy one. But that law was not much enforced.

Le Havre's main cotton trade was with New Orleans, at the mouth of the Mississippi River. So that is where Le Havre ships took most German emigrants. But the Southern climate and life-style were not very appealing to these new immigrants. So many of them headed toward cities up the Mississippi, or headed to farms west.

Emigrants also began to leave Germany through the port at Bremen. In 1827, the city arranged a treaty with the United States, making both trade and immigration easier and less expensive. In 1830, Bremen opened a major new transatlantic port at nearby Bremerhaven.

More and more emigrants from northern Germany, especially Hanover and Westphalia, began to head down the Weser River Valley to Bremen. Local states barred regular steamboat traffic on the Weser, so most emigrants traveled overland. Families would often rent a large wagon in a city like Stuttgart to transport them and their goods to Bremen. The wagoneer would then return home, hopefully with a load of goods from the port city.

Emigrants were still at risk in port, but Bremen dealt with the problems head-on. By 1855 the city had developed an admirable system for handling the thousands of emigrants. When they arrived in Bremen, emigrants were met by licensed agents. The agent's job was to see that the newcomers arrived safely at the port, without being robbed or cheated. Emigrants were housed in a government-provided dormitory, offering food and lodging for a small charge. Bremen even published a special newspaper, the *Deutsche Auswanderer Zeitung*. This warned emigrants of frauds and swindles and told them where to go for information both in Bremen and in American cities such as New York. With its reputation as a safe port, Bremen attracted increasing numbers of German emigrants.

Early Bremen ships generally sailed to Baltimore. There they picked up tobacco and cotton from the mid-South, especially Virginia and the Carolinas, for the return voyage. In fact, tobacco dealers turned into immigration agents, trying to get human cargo for their ships. Later Bremen ships sailed to all the main American ports. Bremen was even sometimes laughingly called a suburb of New York City.

Seeing Bremen's success, the old Hanseatic port of Hamburg, just to the east on the Elbe River, also entered the emigrant trade. Emigrants themselves decided the issue, by showing up in Hamburg looking for passage across the Atlantic. In fact, packet ships—ships that sailed on a regular schedule rather than waiting for a full load of cargo—sailed regularly from Hamburg. But there were too few of them to handle the number of emigrants wanting passage. And, unlike Le Havre and Bremen, Hamburg had no regular trade arrangements with American ports, and therefore had few cargo ships.

But large numbers of packet ships did sail from Great Britain to America. So the Hamburg merchants set up a regular steamship route to the port of Hull, on England's east coast, three days away. From Hull, emigrants took a three-day trip by canal or train to the main Atlantic port of Liverpool. Though passage was more expensive on a packet ship than on a cargo ship, emigrants saved the cost and physical hardship of waiting in port.

Soon the Hamburg-Hull-Liverpool route became widely used, not only by Germans but also by Scandinavians. As in Bremen, emigrants were closely watched in Hamburg. They could buy all the necessary tickets from German agents in Hamburg, and English-speaking German guides took them all the way to Liverpool.

By the early 1830s, travel barriers on the Rhine were removed, and ports like Antwerp, in Belgium, and Rotterdam, in the Netherlands, took some of the German emigrant traffic. But most German emigrants continued to travel through Le Havre, Bremen, and Hamburg, all of which came to have packet ships in addition to cargo ships. The spread of railroads in the 1850s made it even easier for German emigrants to reach these ports.

Swimming Coffins

The emigrant ships were, alas, still quite unsafe for human beings. In the holds of cargo ships that carried tobacco or cotton eastbound, temporary partitions were removed and bunks installed. This was the area called "steerage" because it lay near the ship's steering mechanism. Into these holds, emigrants were crammed by the hundreds. The ships were grossly overloaded. There was no privacy—men, women, and children all were housed together in steerage. Passengers with the money to travel first-class had more comfortable accommodations, though still rough by today's standards.

On cargo ships, immigrants generally had to provide and cook their own food. Even where food was provided, there was too little of it, and that was generally spoiled. On the Bremen ship *Johanna*, one passenger reported:

> After two weeks the potatoes gave out; the peas were musty, the meat and butter spoiled and had to be thrown into the sea. The passengers lived on hard branny bread, prunes and watery barley soup. In New York, the cook jumped ship.

Sanitation was primitive and water was scarce. Immigrants emptied their own chamber pots and had to provide their own bedding. In calm weather, immigrants might be sent up on deck for fresh air, but in stormy weather they were kept in the stinking hold. Then as the ship pitched and rolled, they were thrown about, sometimes breaking bones in the process.

In these conditions, diseases like cholera and smallpox flourished. The result was that many of these vessels became, in the words of an 1853 New York City newspaper editorial, "damned plague ships and swimming coffins." Few ships made the westbound passage without at least one death. Some had many more, like the *Howard* out of Hamburg which, in its 96-day voyage to New York, lost 37 out of its 286 passengers to cholera. Over a third of the survivors were too ill to walk off the ship and had to be carried off. As Freidrich Kapp, himself a German immigrant, said in an 1867 report to an immigrant aid society, "If crosses and tombstones could be erected on the water, the routes of the emigrant vessels from Europe to America would long since have assumed the appearance of crowded

The German ports of Bremen and Hamburg (shown here) developed whole "emigrant villages," where America-bound travelers could be housed and kept safe from robbers while waiting for their ships. (National Archives)

cemeteries." Ships from France and Britain were even worse and had a far higher death rate than those from Hamburg and Bremen.

Some Americans were concerned about the plight of the immigrants. They formed immigrant aid societies, wrote petitions, and pressured legislators to better conditions on immigrant ships. Some European cities like Bremen also urged reform. In 1847 Congress passed a new law specifying that each passenger was to have at least 14 square feet of space, with bunks at least 6 feet long and 18 inches wide. The new law also required that men and women be given separate entrances, bunk areas, and toilets. But even when the laws were observed, the ships were still overcrowded, and passengers were sometimes forced to sleep in hallways or even in crude shacks nailed together on deck. It would be decades before conditions improved enough to significantly lower the immigrant death rate.

The trip westbound across the Atlantic continued to be a long one. From Liverpool it took at least 35 days; from Bremen or Hamburg more like 50 or 60. As shipowners competed with each other for immigrant passengers, the cost of passage went down sharply in the first half of the 19th century. A steerage trip from Britain to America in 1819 might cost 10 to 12 pounds; by 1832, an emigrant would more likely pay 6 pounds on a packet or 4 pounds on a cargo ship. The fare from Le Havre and other major ports was also cut by half in the same period.

The ocean journey itself began to improve greatly only in the 1860s, as steamships started to replace the old sailing ships. These gradually cut the length of the westbound journey from two to four months to more like two to three weeks. They also offered better food and sleeping quarters. But old sailing ships, with their terrible conditions, operated until late in the century, providing cheap passage for the poorest immigrants.

Arrival

In American ports, German immigrants faced many of the same hazards they faced in European ports. Most of these newcomers, called *greenhorns*, did not speak English. Many of them were also straight off the farm. Not used to city ways, they were easy prey for thieves and con men, who haunted the docks.

It was partly to protect immigrants from such hazards that the United States established regular inspection of immigrants on arrival. The other, more important, reason was that many Americans were nervous about the large number of immigrants, so they wanted to screen out "undesirable" ones. From the mid-19th century on, immigrants arriving at any American port had to be checked by immigration inspectors before they were allowed to enter the country. First-class passengers were given only a brief inspection on board ship. But passengers from steerage, where most immigrants traveled, were given more careful inspection.

Most cities, such as Baltimore, Philadelphia, and New Orleans, had small immigration stations. But as New York increasingly became a focus for European immigration, special arrangements were made to handle immigrants. An inspection station was set up at the tip of Manhattan Island, in an old fort turned musical theater: Castle Garden. From 1855 through the 1890s, most immigrants arriving in New York City passed through the Castle Garden immigration inspection station.

In 1892 the inspection station was moved out into New York Harbor to Ellis Island. Unfortunately, just after it was finally completed, Ellis Island burned completely to the ground, destroying all of the Castle Garden and Ellis Island immigration records from 1855 to 1897. Because of that, many German-Americans today who want to learn about their 19th-century immigrant ancestors have a hard time trying to trace their

arrival. Ellis Island was rebuilt, and from 1900 to the 1930s saw most immigrants passing through New York City.

Immigration inspectors were supposed to keep out people with criminal records, mental illness, or any other illness, such as heart disease or tuberculosis, that might make them a "public charge"—that is, someone needing welfare support. Immigrants with certain serious contagious diseases were absolutely barred from entering the country. Among these diseases were trachoma, an eye disease that causes eventual blindness, and favus, a highly contagious scalp disease. Often far too many people arrived to be processed in a day, so immigrants sometimes had to spend one or more nights sleeping on rough benches at Castle Garden or cage-like wire bunks at Ellis Island.

If not allowed to enter, immigrants were sent back to Europe at the shipping line's expense. There they were deposited back in port, far poorer than they had started and no longer citizens of any state. But, in fact, relatively few people were sent back during the Castle Garden years. These were the years of the so-called Old Immigration, from Northern Europe, including Germany.

The later Ellis Island years were the years of the New Immigration, primarily from Southern and Eastern Europe. After the turn of the 20th century, immigration inspection gradually became stricter. For example, immigrants were often required to show a certain amount of money, to have a sponsor in this country, and later to be able to read and write. After 1885, immigrants faced a contract labor law that banned recruiting of immigrants to fill American jobs. So immigrants could not say they had a firm job waiting for them. But neither could they say they had no job, for then they might be seen as possible "public charges." Treading a fine line—difficult, since most spoke no English and had to communicate through interpreters—they had to say only that they had "good hopes" of a job. Medical examinations were also far more strict.

But Germans were not much affected. Being Northern European Protestants and often skilled people, they were considered highly desirable immigrants. At Ellis Island, the immigration inspection was directed more at the "less desirable" New Immigrants. In fact, when the United States set up a quota system for immigrants in the 1920s, it highly favored Germans and other people of the Old Immigration, while severely restricting others. As a result, many new German immigrants were barely inspected at all, but simply passed on into the United States.

Immigrants sent back to Europe suffered a heartbreaking fate. To help prevent that—and also to spare shipping lines the expense of providing return passage for free—the German ports of Bremerhaven and Hamburg early began to provide vaccinations and medical inspections in Europe. Though immigrants could still get a disease on board ship, fewer were likely to be turned back at Ellis Island.

Later the United States made such European inspections the rule. After the 1930s, therefore, fewer people had to pass through Ellis Island. The inspection station saw heavy use again after World War II, when many refugees sought a new home in America. Ellis Island was finally closed in 1954, though in recent years it has been restored as a shrine to America's immigrants and reopened to the public.

Heading West

On arrival in America, many German immigrants settled in or near the ports where they entered—New Orleans, Baltimore, Philadelphia, New York, or Galveston, for example. But for many the journey took them farther west.

In the days before the railroads, new immigrants followed the main land and water routes. Germans arriving in New Orleans sometimes worked their way up the Mississippi River to cities such as St. Louis or Cincinnati, or went west to Texas or beyond. Those arriving in Baltimore tended to follow Daniel Boone's path through the Cumberland Gap into the Kentucky or Ohio country, or on into the upper Mississippi Valley.

But in the first half of the 19th century more and more immigrants followed the main route west, along the Hudson and Mohawk river valleys through upstate New York. After 1825 the Erie Canal linked these rivers with the Great Lakes. Water travel being far easier than overland travel in this period, New York quickly became the favored port of arrival.

Gradually railroads were cut through the Appalachians. Then immigrants arriving in New York City more often went west through the mountains by train, especially to the Ohio and upper Mississippi rivers. Special trains, "stretched to the length of a monstrous serpent," carried immigrants by the thousands into the heart of the country. Sometimes the trains could not handle them all, and newcomers would have to camp out in the open or in abandoned buildings before they could find westbound transporation. These immigrants headed beyond the Mississippi generally gathered at St. Louis. There immigrant pioneers could buy the wagons, horses, and provisions they needed for crossing the Great Plains.

After 1869, railroads spanned the continent from the Atlantic to the Pacific. Then immigrants generally took trains to the West. Like the port cities, the 19th-century trains were crawling with con men and thieves.

By the 1920s, immigrants like this German family arriving at Ellis Island were each given a label to pin on their coats to ensure that they caught the right train for their destination. (By Lewis W. Hine, New York Public Library)

Because of that, Germans recruited to settle and work in America were often met by special state or company agents, who guided them to their destinations. Later immigrants passing through Ellis Island were generally grouped by train, with each immigrant bearing a label indicating his or her destination. But the only sure guard against such hazards was knowledge and experience. Since German immigrants were generally better educated than most other immigrants in the late 19th and early 20th centuries, they encountered fewer problems with robberies and fraud than some other immigrant groups.

By the 1920s and 1930s, the age of the great transatlantic liners had arrived. Steerage quarters still left much to be desired, but they were far better than those on the old "swimming coffins." Also, many more immigrants in this period were refugees with some money. They could take advantage of the more attractive first- and second-class quarters on the ocean liners. And, as U.S. immigration quotas sharply cut immigration, ships were generally far less crowded.

Modern German immigrants, of course, generally arrive in America by air, covering in just a few hours a distance that used to take months.

5

Colonial Times

. . . those people who may let themselves be talked into . . . the voyage [to America] by the thieves of human beings are the biggest fools if they really believe that in America or Pennsylvania roasted pigeons are going to fly into their mouths without their having to work for them.

Gottlieb Mittelberger,
Journey to Pennsylvania

The first German immigrant to North America may have been a sailor named Tyrker. Norse sagas tell of how the Vikings sailed west across the North Atlantic in about 1001 A.D. There "Tyrker the German" found grapevines, causing the Vikings to name the place Vinland (Wineland). From the descriptions, Vinland would probably have been on the northeast coast of North America, somewhere between Labrador and the Hudson River. But, the sagas tell us, the Vikings left within the year. After that it would be over five centuries before we hear of Germans in America.

Meanwhile, in 1492, Christopher Columbus discovered the new land from the mid-Atlantic, thinking it was Asia. Another explorer, Amerigo Vespucci, believed that the new-found land was truly a new continent. It was a German mapmaker, Martin Waldseemüller, who first suggested that the land "be named after Americus" (his version of "Amerigo"); on second thought he changed that to "America, since both Europe and Asia derived their names from women."

Early Settlers

German scholars were much interested in this America and published many books about European discoveries there. Though the German states were not sending their own expeditions to America, some Germans joined parties sent by other nations. A few may have been in the early Spanish and Portuguese settlements. Some German Protestants joined a short-lived

French Huguenot settlement at Port Royal, in what is now South Carolina, in 1607.

Some Germans were also among the British who founded Jamestown, Virginia, in 1607. They were such hardworking people that, in a letter to England, Captain John Smith asked that more Germans and Poles be sent to him—"carpenters, husbandmen, gardiners, fishermen, blacksmiths, masons." He was quite clear that he did not want more of the English "Adventurers that never did know what a day's work was."

These early Germans disliked British treatment of the Native Americans. Some Germans eventually left the Jamestown colony to live with the tribe of Chief Powhatan. As a result, some of the British, including John Smith, came to call them the "damned Dutch"—from *Deutsch*, or German. More Germans arrived in the region later, skilled workers of various sorts. Among them were some who became tobacco farmers and winemakers in the colony of Virginia.

Some Germans also came to America with the Dutch. Peter Minuit (born Minnewit), director of the New Netherlands colony, was actually a German from the Rhineland. On his arrival in 1626, Minuit reportedly bought the island of Manhattan from the Native Americans for 60 Dutch guilders (about $24). There he founded the city of New Amsterdam. Near the tip of Manhattan Island, Minuit built a fort. The site is now called the Battery and faces the Statue of Liberty in New York Harbor. Later immigrants would land nearby, after passing through the Castle Garden or Ellis Island immigration stations. The New Netherlands colony thrived, but in 1632 Minuit was forced to resign as the director after a disagreement over the large Hudson River land grants.

Within a decade Minuit returned to America, this time with colonists from Sweden. At his suggestion, the party—mostly Scandinavian, but including some Germans—headed for the region between the New Netherlands and Virginia colonies. They were the first European settlers on the lower Delaware River, settling parts of present-day Pennsylvania, Delaware, New Jersey, and Maryland. The Swedish colonies were taken over by the Dutch in 1655. The Dutch territories, in turn, were taken over by the British in 1664, and New Amsterdam became New York.

Even so, another German briefly acted as governor of New York. In 1688, Britain's Catholic king, James II, was overthrown. He was replaced by new Protestant rulers—William, king of the Netherlands, and Mary, his English queen. At this, many people of New York, mostly Protestants, rebelled against the old Catholic governor of the colony. In

German-born Peter Minuit, as Governor of the colony of New Netherlands, bought Manhattan Island from the local Native Americans.
(Library of Congress)

1689, while waiting for word from the new King William, the popular party elected a "committee of safety" for the settlement's protection. They chose as their leader Jacob Leisler, a German immigrant from Frankfurt-am-Main, who had come to America originally as a soldier for the Dutch West Indies Company. In 1690, with British colonies under attack by the French, Leisler called a council of the governors of the British colonies, to plan their common defense.

The divisions between the aristocrats and the popular party were deep, however. In the end, when King William's new governor arrived, the aristocratic party won his favor, and Leisler was hanged. The British Parliament restored Leisler's name and the family's fortune a few years later, but the deed was done.

Leisler was the first American leader elected to speak for the people against the aristocrats. And he called the first congress of the American colonies, setting the model for the Continental Congress called by the American revolutionaries less than a century later.

Other Germans, too, contributed to these early colonies. A few we know by name and reputation. Dr. Hans Kierstede, from Magdeburg, was New Amsterdam's first physician and surgeon, arriving in 1638. Augustin Herrman was the first immigrant to become a naturalized citizen under Maryland's 1666 law. His name survives in the small town of Port

Herrmann. A settler from Cologne gave his name to Hack's Point, Maryland. Swiss-German Peter Fabian was part of an English expedition to explore the area of the Carolinas in 1663. Another German explorer, John Lederer, was sent by the Virginia governor to explore the same region in 1669-1670. A German from Württemberg reportedly traveled west from the Mississippi into what is now Texas with an ill-fated French party under La Salle in 1687.

Germantown

The Pastorius party of German immigrants arrived in Philadelphia on October 6, 1683. The arrival of these Krefelders from Frankfurt-am-Main is the date commonly celebrated as the beginning of German-American history.

The Frankfurt Company had bought 25,000 acres and the settlers themselves 18,000 more, six miles north of Philadelphia—then a small town only two years old. Beyond the few roughly constructed homes, Pastorius wrote, "The rest [of Philadelphia] was woods and brushwoods, in which I lost my way several times in an area no greater than that between the river bank and the house of my friend . . ."

They called their settlement *Deutschstadt*—in English, Germantown. The early days were hard. While a permanent home was being built, Pastorius lived in a shack 30 by 15 feet, with oil-soaked paper covering the windows. As he later wrote, ". . . in the early days [Germantown] could well be called Armentown, the 'city of the poor.'"

Germantown did not remain poor for long. Most of the new immigrants were skilled people, many of them weavers. Germantown farmers raised flax for the weavers' looms. Soon Germantown's fine woven goods were being exported beyond Philadelphia. Some German immigrants—true to a tradition that stretched back to the Romans—established vineyards. Later, when a court seal was designed for Germantown, it showed a weaver's shuttle, a flax blossom, and a vine.

Other Germans, many of them sectarians, followed. They, too, were skilled people—carpenters, locksmiths, shoemakers, tailors, and more weavers. Following a common colonial pattern, many farmed part-time to help provide food for their families. Some set up small shops. At least one had set up a brewery and a saloon by 1695. Even some who had arrived as servants became prosperous enough to own land in Germantown.

As new immigrants joined the community, Germantown expanded to the north. Pastorius was one of the town's early officeholders and also a teacher. From 1698-1700 he taught at the Quaker School in Philadelphia. Later he headed Germantown's own school, which provided education for children during the day and for adults at night.

Few other German settlers wanted to serve as town officers. Because Mennonites and some other sectarians believed that government and religion should be separated as much as possible, they were not required to hold office. The community was so peaceful that the local court, summoned into session every six weeks, often had no cases waiting to be heard.

But Germantown residents had very strong feelings on one political issue: slavery. In 1688 some of Germantown's most prominent residents made a formal written protest against the selling of human beings—the first such action taken in the North American colonies. Some 17 years later, their anti-slavery view was adopted by the Quaker movement as a whole.

In keeping with their pacifist beliefs, many Mennonite and Quaker settlers also had friendly relations with local Native Americans. Colonist Daniel Falckner wrote in 1702: "To secure and keep their confidence, we

Francis Daniel Pastorius led the first party of German immigrants to Germantown, Pennsylvania, where he served as teacher and town officer, and also organized the country's first formal protest against slavery.
(Library of Congress)

let them come to our houses, and do not let them go without eating and drinking, and when they come in the evening we give them permission to lie by the fire and so when we go to them they are more kindly and hospitable."

Germantown retained its ethnic character for many years. German was the language of the home, street, store, school, and church. German books and newspapers were printed there, or imported from abroad. Germantown even had its own paper mill, the first in the British colonies. It was established in 1690 by Wilhelm Ruttinghausen and his family from the Netherlands. As late as 1793, when President George Washington attended a Reformed Church in Germantown, the service was given in German.

After 1707, Germantown became part of the city of Philadelphia. But the settlement continued to act as a magnet for other settlers from Germany and Switzerland, especially Mennonites. Between 1717 and 1732 about 3,000 of them followed Pastorius' lead to Pennsylvania.

Later, in the 19th century, as the city of Philadelphia moved out to engulf it, Germantown would lose its distinctive ethnic character. Then names like Schumacher, Kunders, and Ruttinghausen often became Anglicized—to Shoemaker, Conrads, and Rittenhouse.

The First Palatines

In 1708-09, a second major group came to America: the Palatine Germans. The British brought these immigrants to work in New York's pine forests, supplying tar and pitch for Britain's navy. They hoped that the German settlers would help secure the New York frontier against attacks by the local Iroquois tribes.

Over 2,500 Palatine Germans arrived in New York in April 1710, led by a minister, Josua von Kocherthal. Most of them settled in the mid-Hudson Valley. There they founded several villages, including Newburgh, and set to work producing tar and pitch. Unfortunately the governor charged with supporting them died, and a new British government abandoned the project in 1711. This left the Palatines on their own, without promised supplies and financial help.

At first, the settlers faced extreme hardships. Their British landlords and governors had little sympathy with their plight and the Palatines resented their rule. Within a year or two many of the Palatine Germans had moved farther out on the frontier, away from British control.

They pushed north along the Hudson, west along the Mohawk, and south of there along the Schoharie. In these river valleys, they founded many of the first European settlements, and were the first to clear and farm prime bottomlands. The Palatine villages so dominated these valleys that parts were called the "German flats." Towns like Mannheim, Oppenheim, and Herkimer, with their solid stone houses, still recall these early German settlements.

Some of this first wave of Palatine Germans stayed in New York City. Over 40 immigrant children, some orphaned on the transatlantic crossing, were signed over as apprentices—actually redemptioners. One, John Peter Zenger, learned the printing trade and founded his own newspaper in New York City. Later a libel trial involving Zenger established the principle of freedom of the press. That freedom was later written into the Bill of Rights of the Constitution of the new United States.

The rest of these early Palatines settled elsewhere on the Atlantic coast and especially in Pennsylvania. Penn's idealistic colony would continue to be a magnet, as settlers sent word back to Germany of the attractive religious haven they had found.

Extending the Frontier

These settlers were followed by other Palatines during the 18th century. In 1714, some German families—chosen for their mining and engineering skills—were brought to the colony of Virginia, where they founded the town of Germanna, near modern Fredericksburg. Other German immigrants later joined them, but the governor's iron mining project was not successful. Like the Palatine Germans in New York State, those in Virginia had by the mid-18th century moved out of British control, settling a new Germantown.

Over 600 Palatine Germans were sent to the Carolinas, selected by the "Lord Proprietors" of the colony as skilled, healthy, hard-working individuals. There they founded the town of New Bern. Unfortunately, their supplies ship was lost to French privateers, and the local Native American tribes severely attacked their town. Eventually most left New Bern for other parts of North Carolina.

In the 1730s over a thousand exiled Protestants, forced out of Catholic Salzburg, in Austria, emigrated to Georgia. In 1734, the first party settled the town of Ebenezer, north of Savannah. A later party was

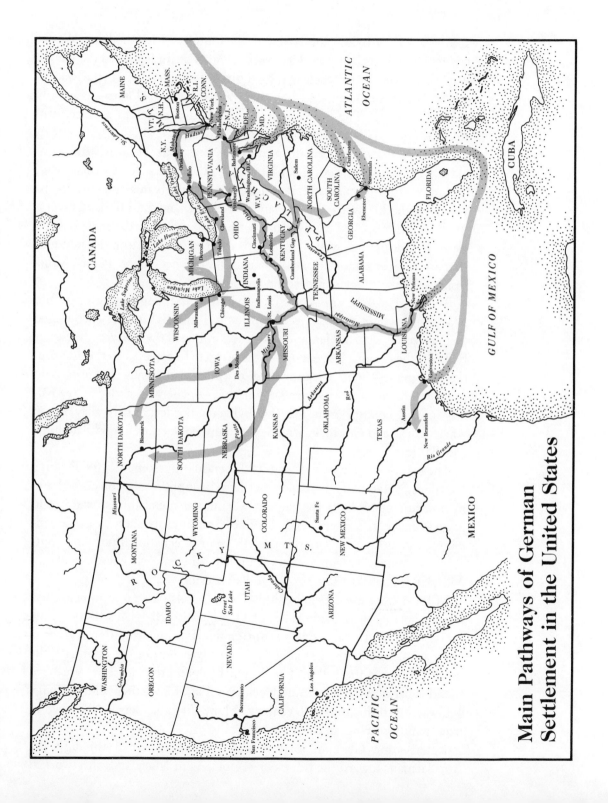

Main Pathways of German Settlement in the United States

accompanied by Briton John Wesley, the founder of Methodism. Wesley was much influenced by the Germans' friendly attitude toward the Native Americans, and also by their hymn-singing. Though settled in the heart of the South, these Germans—like their kin in other colonies—generally opposed slavery. The Salzburgers established themselves as successful silkgrowers, exporting their goods to Europe.

Many of the new German immigrants began to settle in rural areas outside Philadelphia, too. They generally headed first for Germantown, then moved out into southern and eastern Pennsylvania, notably in the valleys of the Delaware, Susquehanna, Lehigh, and Cumberland rivers. As those regions filled up, German settlers moved toward Pennsylvania's western frontier as well. By the time of the American Revolution, Benjamin Franklin estimated, one out of every three Pennsylvania residents was of German descent.

By the 1730s Pennsylvania Germans had begun moving into Maryland, where the colony's proprietor, Lord Baltimore, encouraged them to settle. British plantation owners dominated the lowlying tidewater region—the region close enough to the ocean to be affected by the tide. But the Germans—who disapproved of plantation-style farming and preferred to work family farms themselves—generally settled in the rolling inland country near the Pennsylvania border. There they raised wheat, corn, and livestock, which they supplied to cities like Philadelphia and Baltimore.

They were joined in the mid-18th century by some 2,800 Palatine Germans. Many of these new settlers brought craft, business, and manufacturing skills to the region, working as metalsmiths, wagon and harness makers, tanners, and the like. Immigrants such as these contributed greatly to Baltimore's growth as an international port and commercial center. Germans also founded other nearby settlements in Maryland, such as Hagerstown and Frederick.

In the 1730s some Pennsylvania Germans also began to move father inland, notably to the wide Valley of Virginia. Scotch-Irish settlers led the early trek southward into frontier lands, but the Pennsylvania Germans—among them many German-Swiss—came to dominate the northern part of the valley. The Scotch-Irish and the Germans tended to found separate villages. Some German villages kept their old language and ways until the mid-19th century. Many Virginia Germans worked in iron manufacturing and charcoal burning.

Later some German settlers also moved eastward through the Appalachians toward the tidewater region. As in Maryland, they worked their farms with their own hands, growing produce for nearby towns and cities, rather than adopting the slaveholding pattern of the great tobacco plantations.

Though the early German settlement in Carolina had not prospered, the British colonial governors still tried to attract new settlers to the frontier. Some 12,000 German-Swiss settlers came to Purysburg, South Carolina. There many worked making silk or making wine from new vineyards. Other new immigrants settled along the Savannah River, in the area they called Saxe-Gotha, today South Carolina's Orangeburg and Lexington counties. As early as 1766, such colonists formed a charitable and social group called the German Friendly Society, in Charleston, South Carolina.

Meanwhile, Pennsylvania Germans continued to move out on the frontier, into the Shenandoah Valley and south into the Carolinas. In 1753 a large group of Moravians from Bethlehem, Pennsylvania, bought land in the Piedmont area of North Carolina. There they founded Bethany and Salem, among many other towns in the region.

A few German immigrants also went to the French colonies centered on New Orleans. In 1721, the French government sent 250 Germans to settle in the lower Mississippi Valley. The new immigrants settled north of New Orleans, in an area that came to be known as the "German Coast."

A few German settlers were also found in New England. They founded Waldoboro in Maine, and several towns in northwestern Massachusetts, including Adasdorf, Bernardsdorf, and Leyden.

Life on the Land

For settlers on the land, life in America was filled with hard work. Forests had to be cleared and fields fenced. As Gottlieb Mittelberger commented, Europeans "learn from experience that oak tree stumps are just as hard in America as they are in Germany." On a German farm, *everyone* pitched in, including the women and children. British settlers sometimes criticized German women as being "unfeminine" for doing farm work. The results, however, were admirable.

The settlers' houses were sturdy and simple. On first arrival, German settlers—like other pioneers—generally lived in a kind of cave dug out of earth, and then progressed to a log cabin. But as soon as they could, they would build a solid stone house, often with a tile roof. Such houses were often two stories high, with the lower story built into the side of a hill. Generally the houses were heated with wood stoves, rather than heat-wasting fireplaces. That way, as Philadelphia physician Benjamin Rush commented, "twice the business is done by every branch of the family, in knitting, spinning, and mending farming utensils than is done in houses where every member of the family crowds near to a common fireplace, or shivers at a distance from it."

Often a spring near the house served as a natural refrigerator, and a separate bakehouse and storage cellar were set up close by. Most German colonial farms included an orchard, a beehive, and a kitchen garden growing produce for family use, especially cabbage and turnips. German settlers are credited with being the first to cultivate asparagus and cauliflower in America. Germans, especially Pennsylvania Dutch, placed bright, simple decorations—such as an image of a peacock, a dove, or a tulip—on almost everything they made and used, from their red earthenware pottery and tables to their quilts and chests.

The large barns of the German settlers were modeled on those in Bavaria's Black Forest region. They were solidly built two-story wood frame barns, resting on firm stone foundations. They were often painted and decorated in bright yellows or reds. The lower story housed the stables, while the grain was threshed and stored on the floor above and in lofts under the high-pitched roof. Heavy ramps allowed wagons to be driven directly onto the second story to load or unload grain. Farmers kept their livestock carefully housed—so carefully, in fact, that some charged they had better conditions than the humans. A late-18th-century French visitor noted that in the Pennsylvania Dutch (German) settlements, "The houses are small, and kept in very bad order; the barns are large, and in very good repair."

And, indeed, the Germans did live simply. The first generation—that is, those who had been born in Germany—had the hardest time. That was especially true for redemptioners, who worked for years paying off their passage money only to start their free life with almost nothing to their names. But the second and later generations generally prospered through careful spending—critics called it penny-pinching—and hard work. Benjamin Franklin once commented that the English seemed to be less hardworking in the new world than in the old, "but it is not so with the German laborers; they retain their habitual industry and frugality they bring with them, and, receiving higher wages, an accumulation arises that makes them all rich." A governor of Pennsylvania even credited German "Industry and Frugality" with making Pennsylvania the most prosperous of "any of his Majesty's Colonys in North America."

German settlers paid special attention to their tools and equipment. To take their fruits, vegetables, and other goods to market in nearby cities, they used a covered wagon, sometimes called "the ship of inland commerce," drawn by four, six, or eight horses. The bottom of the wagon, often painted blue with red gear, was sunk in the center to keep the load from shifting on rough roads, and the whole was topped with a hood of white linen. This was the famous Conestoga wagon that America's pioneers would later take with them as they opened up the West.

The Plain People

Religion was important for most German immigrants in colonial times. In the early part of the 18th century, many immigrants were sectarians—Mennonites, Amish, Schwenkfelders, Dunkers, Moravians, and others. In America they were often known as the "Plain People," for their simple style of life and dress.

The Plain People shared many beliefs. They were for nonviolence and against military service, slavery, and participation in government. In this country, those beliefs were generally respected, and they were exempt

The German-built Conestoga wagon (right) became the main vehicle for local hauling, as here on Pennsylvania's Lancaster Turnpike in 1795, or for cross-country pioneering. (Library of Congress)

from military service and from holding political office. Dr. Benjamin Rush urged his fellow British settlers:

> Above all, cherish with peculiar tenderness, those sects among them [the Germans] who hold war to be unlawful—Relieve them from the oppression of absurd and unnecessary militia laws . . . Perhaps those German Sects of Christians among us, who refuse to bear arms for the purpose of shedding human blood, may be preserved by divine providence, as the centre of a circle which shall gradually embrace all the nations of the earth in a perpetual treaty of friendship and peace.

Many of these Plain People, especially in Pennsylvania, settled in tightly knit communities and held so strongly to these beliefs that they survived all pressures to give up their langue, their life-style, and their beliefs. Some of them even yet have kept to their own ways, dressing in the same simple style, following their strict pattern of religious life, and still speaking German—though today with some American words added.

Among the best-known members of these early sectarian immigrants was Christopher Sauer, a Dunker who printed the first German Bible in America and the first German farmer's almanac. He also published a German-language newspaper, *Der Hoch-Deutsch Pennsylvanische Geschichts-Schreiber*, circulated widely among German communities, even as far away as Georgia. Christopher Dock, a Mennonite teacher from Skippack, Pennsylvania, is credited with introducing the blackboard into classrooms, in 1714. He also may have written the first American book on teaching, *Schul-Ordnung*.

Some Moravians had settled in Georgia with the Salzburgers in the mid-1730s. However, the community there did not respect their views on nonviolence and their refusal to bear arms. So they moved to Pennsylvania, especially to the Lehigh River Valley. There they founded several towns and cities, including Bethlehem, named by their protector, Count Zinzendorf. On their first Christmas eve, in 1741, he led the Moravians in the joyous singing of hymns. That love of music and singing remains strong to this day in and around old Moravian settlements, notably in Bethlehem, Pennsylvania, and Salem, North Carolina.

Many Moravians were also very active as missionaries, living among the Native American tribes on the frontier. By 1755 missionaries such as David Zeisberger, John Hackewelder, and Christian Post had established missions far into Ohio country, beyond the frontier. These missionaries respected the Native Americans' culture and translated Christian religious works into their languages. They successfully converted many Native Americans to Christianity—and to pacifism. Unfortunately that would leave the new converts open to slaughter later by less "loving" settlers.

One result of this was that the Moravians and the early German settlers generally had an extraordinary relationship with the Native American peoples of the East. Lutheran Johann Conrad Weiser, who had led the Palatine Germans into the Schoharie Valley in 1713, sent his son, Conrad, to live with the local Mohawk tribe to learn their language fully. Later, when he moved to Pennsylvania, Conrad was able to act as ambassador between the Pennsylvania colony and the Native American league. On his death, a Seneca chief mourned Conrad as "one-half Indian," lamenting that "since his Death we cannot so well understand one another."

The Church People

But, after the first wave, the majority of German immigrants were Church People—that is, they belonged to one of the major churches, generally Lutheran or Reformed. While sectarians often traveled to America with their pastor, most Church People did not. At first, many had no minister to help them form a proper congregation and build a church. Traveling preachers sometimes filled in, but these were unsatisfactory in many ways. As a result, many church groups appealed to Europe for pastors.

The Lutherans were lucky enough to be sent Henry (Heinrich) Melchior Mühlenberg as their pastor. At the age of 31, he arrived in America to lead the Lutheran parishes of Philadelphia, New Hanover, and New Providence, where he found a 50-person congregation worshipping in a barn. By 1745, three years after he arrived, the town of New Providence had a proper Lutheran church. Music was so important to these settlers that, within five years, organs had been imported from Germany. By 1748, Mühlenberg had begun active work toward a Lutheran synod—that is, an organization to govern the Lutheran churches of America. By 1754, German, Dutch, and Swedish Lutheran pastors had formed a synod, which grew and expanded in influence after that. Many of the German Lutheran pastors—including some born in America, such as Henry Mühlenberg's son, Peter—were trained in Germany.

Reverend Henry Melchior Mühlenberg, born and educated in Halle, Germany, helped organize a strong and active network of German Lutheran churches in America. (Denkmal der Liebe und Achtung . . ., Library of Congress)

For his work, Henry Mühlenberg is sometimes called the Father of the American Lutheran Church. Trying to pass on both the German religion and German culture to younger generations, he organized a system of church schools, where subjects were taught in German. For some decades he had considerable success, but gradually the trend toward learning and using English as the main language became overwhelming. As he said late in his life: "God is my witness, I worked against the English as long as I could, but I cannot longer resist."

The German Reformed Church had its own leader in Michael Schlatter. Before he arrived in 1746, most of the nearly four dozen German Reformed congregations in the English colonies were joined with the Dutch Reformed group, the Church of Holland. Schlatter quickly organized the German Reformed Church of America. Like Mühlenberg, he actively set up schools for the young. Also, like Mühlenberg, he was not entirely happy with life in America. He was highly critical of German farmers in frontier Pennsylvania, calling them "the dregs of the people, poor, rude, ignorant of divine things." He charged that they were "so occupied with their rustic labors and domestic affairs" that they failed even to teach religion to their children. He was especially unhappy with the many non-traditional sects that existed in the colonies, especially in Pennsylvania.

Neighborly Relations

Pastorius and many other early Germans in Philadelphia had close and friendly relations with their English neighbors. When Germans were few in number in a village or region, that generally continued to be so. The Germans began to speak English and to attend English-speaking churches and schools.

But many German immigrants formed their own communities, attending German churches and schools and speaking German whenever possible. These Germans tended to have little social contact with their non-German neighbors, except in shops and markets. Then misunderstandings sometimes grew up between them and their mostly English or Scotch-Irish neighbors. Some English-Americans, for example, thought the Germans were too stupid and stubborn to learn English. These people simply failed to see that the people they called "the dumb Dutch" were highly skilled, as their success in the new land clearly showed. The simple fact was that many Germans were proud of their language and hoped to keep it alive in the new land. They resented attempts to force them to use English and—as they thought of it—abandon their heritage.

Immigrants from all over the world—including later waves of Germans—would face this problem in America. It is a problem that has no easy solution. For, though people want to hold on to their roots, they also cannot achieve full success in a new land without adopting the main language of the culture. In the end, of course, all but a few communities of sectarian German-Americans gradually gave up their German language and entered the mainstream of English-American life.

German-American Culture

They did not, however, give up their culture—and through it they began to help shape the culture of America. Pennsylvania German farmer's almanacs included much planting and harvesting information, and also much popular wisdom—proverbs, superstitions, customs, folk tales, and the like. Through such works, Germans helped shape the popular myths and legends of America. That was especially true as the colonies broke away from European control and the colonists began to work together to build a new, independent country.

Germans made special contributions to the musical heritage of America. Gottlieb Mittelberger noted that in mid-18th-century

Pennsylvania "it is still pretty difficult to hear good music." When he brought an organ—probably the first in America—to the German Lutheran Church in Philadelphia, he noted:

> Many people came a great distance, ten, twenty, thirty, forty,
> up to fifty hours' journey, in order to see and hear this organ.
> The number of people listening, standing inside and outside
> the church, German and English, has been estimated at several
> thousand.

The widespread use of music and singing in churches and communities across America owes a good deal to this enthusiasm of the German settlers.

Many Germans were highly educated and contributed to America's intellectual life. Among these descendants of Gutenberg were many printers and publishers. During the 18th century, at least 38 German newspapers found an audience in the American colonies, and a flood of religious works poured from German presses. German bookstores were found in many cities throughout the colonies.

On the other hand, many Germans were quite uneducated—often by choice. Some opposed "too much" education on principle, believing in a simple religious belief and moral code. They also rejected British attempts to provide schooling for their children, mainly because the schools would be taught in English, not German.

To some extent this reflected a division between the Church People and the Plain People. Followers of the Lutheran and Reformed churches often respected education. But many sectarians (the Moravians excepted) generally distrusted education and educated people, including doctors and lawyers, as well as pastors. City and country dwellers also differed on these matters. City dwellers often favored education, while many farmers did not, wondering what would happen to farming if everyone were educated.

As a result, perhaps as many as one out of four German settlers could not read or write. These were, Benjamin Franklin once complained, "the most stupid of their own nation." But, educated or not, German settlers had a strong feeling for democracy. In elections, Franklin granted, "they come in droves and carry all before them."

War on the Frontier

By the middle of the 18th century, German-Americans were settled all along the colonial frontier, most heavily in New York's Hudson,

Mohawk, and Schoharie valleys, in southeastern Pennsylvania, in the long valleys of western Maryland and Virginia, and in the western Carolinas. They held prime farmlands, which would soon supply the needs of the Revolutionary forces.

But in the mid-18th century the British and French were still battling for control of North America. The British firmly held the East Coast of what is now the United States, with the frontier generally running along the line of the Appalachian Mountains. The French held the eastern part of what is now Canada and had been moving from the St. Lawrence River Valley through the Great Lakes into the heart of the country, especially to the Ohio and Mississippi rivers. Various Native American tribes along the frontier had made alliances with either the British or the French.

In the resulting struggle—called the French and Indian War, German-Americans were much exposed. In New York State, Germans in the Mohawk and Schoharie valleys were attacked many times by joint French and Native American war parties. Settlers were killed and scalped, their homes and crops burned. The Mohawk settlers, notably those at German Flats, rallied under Captain Nicholas Herkimer (born Nicolaus Herckheimer) to defend themselves.

Those on the Pennsylvania frontier also suffered. The British sent an expedition west to the French Fort Duquesne, but when they were defeated in 1755, the Pennsylvanians were unprotected. Many frontier settlements were attacked and destroyed, including the Moravian settlement of Gnadenhütten. The pacifists of the town were almost all killed. The result, even in peaceful Pennsylvania, was a call for armed defense.

Among the British frontier forces was a division called the Royal American Regiment, mostly made up of Pennsylvania Germans, commanded by Swiss immigrant Henry Bouquet. A division from Virginia, led by a young George Washington, also included many Germans. These troops fought all along the frontier, not just in what is now the United States, but also in Canada, where the final and deciding battles were fought, giving Britain control of North America after 1763.

In these difficult decades, German-Americans such as Conrad Weiser and Christian Post traveled as ambassadors to the various tribes along the frontier. Weiser also carried on many dangerous and delicate negotiations with tribes from New York south to the Carolinas. Post, a Moravian missionary, worked in the Ohio country, which at the time included western Pennsylvania. He converted many Native Americans to Christianity and pacifism, and married a Delaware woman. Post convinced a number of Ohio tribes to break their alliance with the French and cease fighting. The

French then abandoned Fort Duquesne—a key site on the Ohio River—to the British. The site was renamed Fort Pitt (modern Pittsburgh) after British Prime Minister William Pitt.

Looking West

After the war, the British made treaties with the Native American tribes, barring settlement west of a specified line, running roughly along the Appalachians. The region beyond that line was then simply known as "the West." Despite the treaties, a few missionaries, trappers, and explorers moved beyond the mountains, notably into Ohio and Kentucky.

German-Americans were among the earliest settlers to reach the rich lands of Kentucky. The figure most associated with Kentucky, Daniel Boone, is generally considered English. But he may have had some German background, as several early German-American writers claimed. Boone came from Pennsylvania Dutch country, reportedly spoke German fluently, went to school with Germans, and had many German friends.

Just before the Revolutionary War, settlers began to push west, among them many German-Americans and, most notably, Daniel Boone, who grew up in Pennsylvania Dutch country and may even have been partly of German background. (Library of Congress)

But even before Boone pushed his Wilderness Road through the Cumberland Gap—a break in the Appalachians—German-Americans had explored Kentucky. Michael Stoner (born Steiner) and another hunter named Harrod founded Harrodsburg in 1774, a year before Boone founded Boonesborough. Even before that, trapper George Yeager (Jäger) had been brought to the Blue Grass country of Kentucky as a prisoner of some Native Americans. He was killed trying to find it again with some fellow explorers from Ohio. Johann Salling lived for many years among the Cherokees, who called him Menou (The Silent One).

Moravian missionaries had been living and working in the Ohio country for several decades by the time of the Revolutionary War. Johann Ludwig Roth, son of a missionary, was the first child of European background to be born in these Ohio settlements, in rebuilt Gnadenhütten in 1773. Such missionaries were not always welcomed in the wilderness. For example, David Zeisberger, a Moravian who converted a number of warriors to pacifism, was the target of several assassination attempts.

The German-American experience during the French and Indian War was a preview of what settlers would face during the Revolution.

6

The New Republic

With the coming of the Revolution, German-Americans faced difficult decisions. Many had, after all, fled Europe to escape from the never-ending wars. Some had just fought a war in the British colonial army, and many were naturalized citizens of Great Britain. And many were firm pacifists, opposed to violence and fighting of any kind.

German Pacifists

Many German-American pacifists tried to avoid taking sides in the war altogether. In some American colonies, pacifists were given the option of paying special taxes or providing a substitute to fight in their stead. Some pacifists who did that were not much bothered otherwise. In some colonies pacifists were required to take an oath of allegiance to the Revolutionary government. Some who did not were forced to leave, often for Canada. But sometimes they were left alone, especially if they gave other support. Many pacifists fed and sheltered Revolutionary soldiers in their own homes. Others provided medical aid. The Moravians of Bethlehem, for example, operated the Good Samaritan hospital for Washington's army at Valley Forge. Such actions were honored. They laid the pattern for modern "conscientious objectors," those who aid soldiers—often at great danger to themselves—though they do not do actual fighting.

Unfortunately, the pacifist Native Americans converted by the Moravians had no such protection or tolerance. The British and the other tribes urged them to join the Loyalist forces, while the Revolutionaries pressed them to go to the American forts. Many pacifist Native Americans were driven from their homes, singing their German hymns, and were later massacred by American militiamen.

German Tories

But many Germans were not pacifists. Some took the British side on principle, finding it extremely difficult to then break their oath of loyalty to the British king. Among the most famous German Tories—that is, British Loyalists—were members of Philadelphia's rich and powerful printing and publishing family, the Sauers.

Some German-Americans fought in the British army. Some were spies for the British, among them two who were hanged in Lancaster, Pennsylvania. But the number of German-Americans who took the British side was relatively small. In fact a smaller proportion of Germans supported the Tories than in the general population.

Many German soldiers *did* fight on the British side, but most of them were imported for the purpose. These mercenaries, the Hessians, fought well, even fiercely, on the British side. Colonial observers of the time noted the Hessians' deadly skill with a bayonet.

But the Americans quickly saw that they had a chance to win some of the Hessians over to their side. They distributed tobacco aswrappers to foreign troops, promising 50 acres of land (more for officers) and full citizenship rights to those who deserted the British for the American side. Hundreds, perhaps thousands, of Hessians did just that. Many more were taken as prisoners of war and later decided to stay on in America, especially after they met German-Americans on the Revolutionary side. Of the 30,000 or so Hessian mercenaries, perhaps a quarter died in the war. Of the rest, some 5,000 to 6,000—perhaps even more—became citizens of the new United States.

Regulars from Germany also fought on the Revolutionary side, though how many and what happened to them is unclear.

German Revolutionaries

The vast majority of Germans had no religious objections to war nor did they support the British on principle. They were certainly not much bothered by the tea tax—that spark of the Revolution—since they did not drink tea. But they very much resented British attempts to lessen the freedoms they had gained in America. As a result, when German-Americans did choose sides in the Revolution, most chose the American side.

Many did more than that—they actively worked toward revolution. In many areas, Germans helped form Committees of Correspondence, the basic organizations of revolutionary supporters in the colonies. In 1776, at the Continental Congress, it was Pennsylvania—with its very large

German population—that cast the deciding vote to adopt the Declaration of Independence.

All through the colonies, in the years just before and during the Revolution, German-Americans worked for the cause of independence. Salzburg immigrant John Adam Treutlen was chosen as a provincial governor of Georgia. German printer Henry Miller (born Heinrich Müller)—who had come to America with Count Zinzendorf—published a Philadelphia newspaper that "fanned the flames of rebellion." This paper, *Der Wöchentliche Philadelphische Staatsboite*, told its readers: "Remember that your forefathers emigrated to America to escape bondage and to enjoy liberty." When, during the war, the British occupied Philadelphia, Miller and others like him, suffered greatly.

German Patriots

One especially active young German-American patriot was Johann Peter Mühlenberg. Though educated in Germany, Peter Mühlenberg's background was "all-American." He was the son of the great Lutheran pastor Henry Mühlenberg; great-grandson of Johann Conrad Weiser, who had led the early Palatine Germans into the Schoharie River Valley; and grandson of Conrad Weiser, who had spent many years as a negotiator with the Native Americans.

A popular Lutheran minister, Peter was a close friend of both Patrick Henry and George Washington. He believed so strongly in the cause of independence that he became chairman of the Committee of Safety and Correspondence in the region near his church in the Shenandoah River Valley. In the end, he gave up his ministry to work more actively for the Revolution.

When, in January 1776, Peter came to preach his final sermon, the church and churchyard were crowded with people come to hear this popular speaker. He did not disappoint them. At the end of his sermon, he announced that "there was a time for preaching and praying, but also a time for battle, and that such a time had now arrived." With that he threw off his minister's robes and revealed his new uniform of colonel in the Continental Army, commanding the Eighth Virginia Regiment.

Peter had also turned recruiter, for out in the churchyard, drums sounded, calling for young men to join the army. Within two days, we are told, over 400 soldiers from the region signed up with Peter's regiment. In fact, Peter Mühlenberg was such an effective recruiter that he was sometimes called away from his regimental leadership to help persuade soldiers to join other regiments in the new Continental Army. Mühlenberg's brigade fought with distinction, notably at the battles of Germantown and Brandywine (where they faced Hessians). He shared the agonies of winter at Valley Forge and the joys of victory at Yorktown. By the end of the war Mühlenberg had risen to the rank of brigadier general, commanding four Virginia regiments.

Not all German-American revolutionary supporters were so highly educated as Peter Mühlenberg. Many were artisans and tradespeople, like Christopher Ludwig. German-born Ludwig supported the move toward independence with words and also with money. Though only, in his own words, "a poor gingerbread baker," he contributed 200 pounds—a huge sum in those days—to buy arms and ammunition for the Revolutionaries.

When war came, Ludwig volunteered, even though he was already 55 years old. At first he worked as a spy for the Americans, posing as a deserter behind British lines. He actively pushed the campaign to persuade Hessians to desert to the American side. As he put it: "Bring the captives [prisoners of war] to Philadelphia, show them our beautiful German churches and homes, let them taste our roast beef, then send them away again to their people and you will see how many will come over to us."

Ludwig's management skills were obvious. They were put to use almost immediately and by 1777 he had been appointed director of baking for the

Peter Mühlenberg was an American-born, German-educated idealist who exchanged his minister's robes for the uniform of a revolutionary in Washington's Continental Army. (Library of Congress)

whole Continental Army. His honesty was clear, too. When asked to supply 100 pounds of bread for every 100 pounds of flour, he replied: "No. Christopher Ludwig does not wish to become rich by the war. He has enough. Out of 100 pounds of flour one gets 135 pounds of bread, and so many I will give." Other bakers, of course, had been supplying 100 pounds of bread, and making a profit on the other 35. George Washington had good reason to call Christopher Ludwig "my honest friend."

The Continental Army

Throughout the colonies, Germans left their farms and shops to become riflemen in the new Continental Army. Companies of German riflemen from Pennsylvania were among the first to reach Commander in Chief George Washington after his call to arms. They were especially welcome because their rifles, improved by their own gunsmiths, were far lighter and more accurate than the standard army musket. (The famous "Kentucky rifle," with which Americans opened up the lands beyond the Appalachians, was actually created by German gunsmiths in Lancaster, Pennsylvania.)

Many German-Americans became officers in the Continental Army. They were joined by experienced officers from Germany, often recruited by Benjamin Franklin, then an American diplomat in Paris. Some served directly under Washington, like Heinrich Lutterloh, who became quartermaster general. Others, such as John Kalb, fought in America with the Revolutionaries' French allies. Some even came over to the American

This painting, which hangs in Pennsylvania's state capitol in Harrisburg, shows General Friedrich von Steuben drilling soldiers at the Continental Army's winter quarters at Valley Forge. (Library of Congress)

side from the British, among them General Friedrich Heinrich (Baron von) Weissenfels and artillery officer Johann Paul Schott.

The most important of the German immigrant officers was Friedrich Wilhelm von Steuben. Baron von Steuben had served in the Prussian army, and he brought a Prussian-style discipline to the American army. Washington quickly made him inspector general of the army, in charge of training and preparation. During the terrible winter at Valley Forge in 1778, Steuben turned the ragtag rebels into an effective army. It was he who wrote the first army manual, called Steuben's Regulations.

Not everyone fully appreciated the contributions of these German officers. Patriot Gouverneur Morris (himself of German background) once complained that these officers were "military fortune hunters . . . men of great ambition who would sacrifice everything to promote their own personal glory—or mere spies . . ." But in general their services were greatly respected and honored.

German-Americans were perhaps proudest of forming George Washington's personal bodyguard during the war. Washington's first personal guard—mostly of English background—were believed to contain some Tories, so he disbanded it. Then in 1778, on the advice of his German-American private aide, he formed an all-German guard called the Independent Troop of Horse. Most of its 53 soldiers and 14 officers were recruited from the Pennsylvania Dutch country, especially Berks and Lancaster counties. This German-speaking troop was led by German-born Major Bartholomew von Heer. Most were discharged at the end of the war, but a dozen served until the end of 1783 and had the honor of escorting Washington to his home at Mt. Vernon, Virginia.

Other individual Germans—many of them unknown and unsung—also made their own contributions to the Revolutionary effort. When Maria Ludwig, a young German-American woman nicknamed Molly, heard that her husband was wounded, she went to join him and nurse him back to health. After that, she followed him and his artillery regiment, bringing water and food and helping to care for the wounded. The grateful soldiers, we are told, often cried out, "Here comes Moll with her pitcher!" At one crucial engagement, when her husband was killed, "Molly Pitcher" took his place at the cannon and rallied the other soldiers nearby.

And it was an unknown Pennsylvania Dutch farmer—perhaps Frederick Leasley or John Jacob Mickley—who smuggled the Liberty Bell out of Philadelphia in a hay wagon, just as the British were entering

German-American Molly Pitcher was acclaimed as a heroine when, after her husband was killed at the Battle of Monmouth in 1778, she took his place at the gun and rallied nearby soldiers.
(By Currier and Ives, Library of Congress)

the city. Moved around to various secret locations, the bell finally was hidden in the basement of the Zion German Reformed Church in Allentown, Pennsylvania. Only after the British left Philadelphia in mid-1778 was the Liberty Bell returned to its proper home.

Fighting on the Frontier

German-American soldiers played perhaps their most crucial role on the Mohawk and Schoharie frontier in New York State. In the early stages of the war, the British had a bold plan to split the Revolutionary forces by taking the Hudson and Mohawk valleys. As part of the plan, a strong British force was to come through the Mohawk Valley and join the rest at Albany.

But they could not fight their way through the American-held Mohawk Valley. Many of the soldiers there and all of the battalion commanders were German, as was their leader, General Nicholas Herkimer. In the summer of 1777, at the Battle of Oriskany, near modern Utica, New York, these rebels stopped a combined force of trained British soldiers and Iroquois. Although the Americans won, their losses were great. At least 200 Palatine Germans—perhaps one out of four—was killed or seriously wounded. General Herkimer himself lost his life. The nearby town of German Flats was renamed Herkimer after him.

The Battle of Oriskany was a key victory for the Revolutionary forces because, as Washington said, it "reversed the gloomy scene" of the war in the northern colonies. By blocking the British advance, these soldiers had made possible the first great American victory at Saratoga some weeks later.

Most other major battles of the war were fought elsewhere in the colonies, but the people of the Mohawk and Schoharie valleys suffered more than most colonists. They were exposed to the fearsome Iroquois, allies of the British. The British paid the Iroquois to bring in the scalps of rebels, and they brought in hundreds, not just from men but also from women and children. In response, many of the local farmers and soldiers became skilled "Indian fighters," helping to protect frontier families. Among them were the Palatine Germans Johann (Hans) Adam Hartman and Nicholas Stoner (Steiner).

German-Americans on the Pennsylvania-Ohio frontier also had their share of action during the war. They joined in several expeditions, of varying success, against Native Americans in the Ohio country.

Shaping the New Republic

At the end of the war, German-Americans returned to their homes, ready to rebuild their lives in a new republic. With them came some thousands of German soldiers, who joined German settlements from New York to the Carolinas.

German-Americans had played an important part in the Revolutionary War. They were considered full partners and honored citizens in the new United States. Though English was clearly the official language of the government, in some states such as Maryland and Pennsylvania, many laws and rulings were routinely translated into German for the benefit of this important group in the population.

German-Americans actively helped shape the new republic. Gouverneur Morris—descendant of German immigrant Jacob Leisler, New York's acting governor in the 17th century—served on the committee that drafted the Constitution. Also active at the Constitutional Convention of 1787 was General Frederick Frelinghuysen, grandson of a Prussian immigrant. In the Mühlenberg family, Peter served the new state of

Pennsylvania as vice president. (Benjamin Franklin was president.) His younger brother, Frederick August Mühlenberg, served as Speaker of the Pennsylvania state legislature, and was the first (and third) Speaker of the United States House of Representatives.

Moving West

After the Revolutionary War, German-Americans became part of another massive change in America—the move west. At war's end, the British and most of their allies, especially the Iroquois of New York State, went north to Canada. No longer bound by British treaties barring settlement beyond the Appalachians, settlers started pouring into the rich lands they had heard so much about from earlier explorers and missionaries.

Daniel Boone's Wilderness Road had already opened the way to the Blue Grass country of Kentucky. And, though during the war Moravian missionaries and their converts had been driven from their Ohio homes, they returned to start again. Hunters and explorers, among them German-Americans, also had made their way into these wilderness lands.

There were three main routes to the west. The northernmost was the Mohawk Trail. Following the Mohawk Valley and the southern shores of the Great Lakes, this was the only easy water-level route through the Appalachian chain between Georgia and the St. Lawrence River. This was the main route taken by the thousands of New Englanders, mostly of British background. But many Palatine Germans also made their way west on the Mohawk Trail—as would many later immigrants fresh from Germany.

The second main westward route ran from Philadelphia and Lancaster out to Fort Pitt, later Pittsburgh, on the Ohio River. Many Pennsylvania Germans favored this route into the Ohio country. At Pittsburgh, they were joined by people from the Mohawk Trail. Beyond Pittsburgh, the easiest route was the river itself. The pioneers built themselves flatboats and sailed down the Ohio, which forms the northern border of Kentucky. In the years just after the Revolutionary War, however, this was dangerous country, as the local Native Americans often ambushed travelers from the banks of the Ohio.

The third main route to the west was Boone's Wilderness Road through the Cumberland Gap into Kentucky. Many German-Americans from

Maryland to the Carolinas favored this route. Before the Ohio country was settled and safe, many Pennsylvania Germans went hundreds of miles out of their way through the Valley of Virginia to take the Wilderness Road.

Whichever route they took, the pioneers were headed for the prime lands surrounding the Ohio River Valley. South of the river lay the rich grasslands of Kentucky and Tennessee. North of it lay the Ohio country. The river itself fed into the great Mississippi at the French city of St. Louis. This whole region—today known as the Midwest—was then called simply "the West."

The paths of German settlement can often be traced by the names of the towns they founded: Berlin, Hanover, Strassburg, Dresden, Frankfort, Winesburg, Potsdam, and other such names from Germany dot the westward migration routes. Settlements of German sectarians—Amish, Dunkers, Mennonites, and others—are often identified with names from the Bible: Bethelehem, Nazareth, Canaan, Goshen, and the like.

The Pioneers

Among the pioneers moving westward were large numbers of Germans. Many Revolutionary War veterans were eligible for land grants in regions like Kentucky. Many Germans had large families and, rather than breaking up the family farm, sent their younger children west to start their own farms. They were joined by many former redemptioners looking for cheap land.

Many of the German pioneers were quite unlike the pacifist Moravians. Some remembered brutal burnings and massacres, and became almost fanatical "Indian fighters." Among these were the Wetzel brothers—Ludwig, Jacob, and Martin—who had lost some of their family in Native American raids during the war. Some organized local defense, like David Ziegler, the commander at Fort Washington, Ohio. (Later, in 1802, when Fort Washington became Cincinnati, Ziegler became its first mayor.) Local Native Americans bitterly resisted invasion, and many pioneers lost their lives in isolated settlements on the frontier. War between the pioneers and the Native Americans continued in the region until 1794 and the successful Ohio campaigns of General Anthony Wayne.

German-American David Ziegler was commander of Fort Washington, built in 1790. Twelve years later, when the settlement became the town of Cincinnati, Ohio (opposite), Ziegler became its first mayor. (Fort Washington: Chromolithography by Ehrgott & Forbriger, Library of Congress, 1857; Cincinnati: Library of Congress, 1802)

Kentucky Country

Records of early Kentucky tell of many German settlements founded "principally [by] families from Pennsylvania—orderly respectable people, and the men good soldiers." Many other Germans came from Virginia, Maryland, the Carolinas, and Georgia. Only gradually did the pioneer settlements take hold and establish secure borders against attack. Yet enormous changes occurred in a single lifetime. As a young man, German-American Henry Crist (born in Virginia as Heinrich Christ) was severely wounded in an attack in wilderness Kentucky. Yet he lived to become a legislator in the new state of Kentucky and later in the United States Congress.

German-Americans were among those who laid out the city of Lexington, Kentucky, in 1781. When Kentucky gained its own court system, one of the first three judges was a German-Scotch-American, George Muter. In 1780, he and other German-Americans helped found Transylvania Seminary, the first college west of the Appalachians. Other German-Americans helped found Kentucky University, which later merged with Transylvania.

With other pioneers, German-Americans pushed through the Kentucky country toward the Mississippi River. This movement accelerated after 1803, when the Americans made the Louisiana Purchase,

buying all French claims to lands on and west of the Mississippi. Since American pioneers were no longer in conflict with the French over that territory, then known as the "Southwest," many more immigrants moved into the region of Tennessee. Among these were very large numbers of Germans, who later helped form the new state of Tennessee, south of Kentucky.

Ohio Country

The other central focus of German-American settlement after the Revolutionary War was the Ohio country—the rich lands north of the Ohio River. While New Englanders of British stock generally settled in northern Ohio, in the so-called Western Reserve region, German-Americans tended to settle in southern Ohio. There they were often joined by new immigrants from Germany.

As in the Kentucky country, many of these pioneers were farmers who cleared land and opened up new regions to the plow. But many others settled in the new frontier towns. Even where the Germans were a minority, their skills and energy—especially in trade and industry—often made them important and influential citizens.

One extraordinary example of the contributions made by German-Americans to the Ohio region is that of Alsace-born Martin Baum. After studying medicine in Baltimore, Maryland, he came to the Ohio country with General Wayne and settled in Cincinnati, on the Ohio River. Starting in 1810, he founded the first iron foundry west of the Appalachians, the first sugar refinery, and the first bank, along with various textile factories and steam mills. With a German partner, Captain Bechtle, he set up a regular shipping business, running sailboats between Cincinnati and New Orleans—the first on the river. Baum was twice mayor of Cincinnati and helped found the city's Western Museum and Cincinnati College. Baum also owned land for and planned the city that became Toledo, Ohio (originally called Port Lawrence).

Baum was far from alone. Other Germans, too, made major contributions to the region. In the Miami Valley, for example, Christopher Wallsmith (Waldschmidt) founded the first paper mill. This provided labor for many newcomers, and laid the basis for many other industries to grow in the area, especially around Dayton and Columbus.

Such business and industry required a great deal of labor, skilled and unskilled. People like Baum and Wallsmith brought to Ohio industrial and scientific experts, as well as workers for the mills and factories. Labor was sometimes in short supply, and many of those who came in the late 18th and early 19th centuries were redemptioners whose contracts had been bought up in the East Coast ports.

German-Americans were also active in the political life of Ohio. In the region of Chillicothe, a former Native American town and the early capital of Ohio, Germans were some of the first pioneer settlers. They were among the first officers of the town and they joined in drafting the state's constitution. Like Baum, they also brought scholars and artists to the region, as visitors and settlers, and helped establish museums and colleges.

New Immigrants on the Frontier

By about 1820, the American frontier was being pushed out to the Mississippi River. Winning their fight with the Native Americans, the pioneers settled the lands past the Falls of the Ohio at Louisville, Kentucky, and eventually all the way down to St. Louis, where the Ohio joins the Mississippi. German-Americans began to settle in St. Louis in large numbers, changing the old French town into a more German city.

About that time, a new wave of German immigration began, with the end of the Napoleonic Wars. Among the new immigrants were many disappointed liberal reformers, often well-educated people, and somtimes people of property and social position in their homeland. Along with them came thousands of more modest immigrants—farmers, artisans, and laborers, both skilled and unskilled.

Many of these new German immigrants headed for the American frontier. Land was cheap and work readily available. The frontier also offered opportunity and freedom. So newly arrived German immigrants often headed from the East Coast ports across the Appalachians or from Gulf of Mexico ports up the Mississippi River to help build the West.

The first of these German immigrants to settle in Missouri were Gottfried Duden, educated as both a lawyer and a doctor, and his brother, Eversmann, a farmer. Gottfried was independently wealthy, so he could hire others to do the hard work of farming. His book on the wonders of America inspired many other Germans to follow him to America.

Those immigrants who came to America with practical skills and experience generally prospered through hard work on the frontier. Unfortunately Gottfried's book attracted many scholars and aristocrats whose backgrounds and skills were unsuited to the rough new West. Many of them came to America with impossibly unrealistic notions of what was involved in clearing and cultivating land. These so-called "Latin farmers" had a rude awakening on the American frontier. Some eventually found their way into towns and cities where their education and skills were useful. But others were broken by the attempt to make a life on the frontier and found themselves trapped on the land. German traveler Frederick Gustorf, who visited St. Louis, Missouri, in 1835, described some of these unfortunates:

> During the day I met many cultured Germans, former farmers, now earning their bread and butter in a very humble way. One German gentleman from the vicinity of Hannover told me several sad stories about the sufferings and hardship of several middle class German families in Missouri and Illinois . . . With their wives, sons, and daughters they live wretched lives. Imagine people from the finest German classes living in miserable huts! . . . They have to eat the plainest of food and do the hardest work in the fields, surrounded by black forests and cut off from society and all the conveniences of life. They live in memory of the sweet past, in contrast with the miserable present, and in contemplation of a sad future . . .

German Colonies

As in the colonial period, some of the new German immigrants came in large groups. Among these were religious groups hoping to found a "New Jerusalem" in America. In 1805 a group led by Johann George Rapp left Württemberg for Pennsylvania, where they founded the communal settlement of Harmony. The Rappists, or Harmonists, also founded a colony in Indiana, on the Wabash River, and another at Economy, in Pennsylvania. The sect banned sex, however, so without children the colonies could not survive in the end. In the 1840s a mystical group called the Community of True Inspiration settled in Ebenezer, New York, and later in Amana, Iowa. Several of these communal societies were quite successful, remaining unified until late in the 19th or early in the 20th century.

In 1839, several groups of Old Lutherans emigrated to America, resisting Prussia's forced merger of the Lutheran and Reformed churches. They formed separate congregations in the several places where they settled, including Buffalo, Milwaukee, and St. Louis.

Some other German groups immigrated to America hoping to found a "new Germany." In about 1830, for example, Paul Follen and Friedrich Münch planned German colonies in the Mississippi Valley. As they explained it:

> We [have] a national idea . . . the foundation of a new and free Germany in the great North American Republic shall be laid by us; we must therefore gather as many as possible of the best of our people about us when we emigrate, and we must at the same time make the necessary arrangements providing for a large body of immigrants to follow us annually, and thus we may be able at least in one of the American territories to establish an essentially German state, in which a refuge may be found for all those to whom, as to ourselves, conditions at home have become unbearable . . .

In 1834, Follen and Münch brought two shiploads of German immigrants, mostly from Hesse, to where the Missouri and Mississippi rivers join. Though this region never became the hoped-for "German state," many more Germans settled nearby—at one point forming 90 percent of the population in the county. Münch himself became a legislator in the new state of Missouri.

Similar movements brought Germans to other states. One brought 130 settlers to Houston by way of Galveston in 1839, though they failed to form a colony. Other similar colonizing societies were formed in Pittsburgh, Cincinnati, and Chicago. Though many of these were unsuccessful as colonies, they served as a focus for further German settlement.

Texas Germans

In 1841 some German settlers in Texas, led by Friedrich Ernst, interested some wealthy German aristocrats in a colony there. The nobles founded a corporation called *Verein zum Schutze Deutscher Einwanderer in Texas*, better known as the *Adelsverein* (the Noblemen's Society). Prince Carl von Solms-Braunfels was sent as the society's head. The community of New Braunfels, Texas, founded in 1844, was named for him.

In the next three years, almost 7,400 German colonists came to Texas, most through Galveston, some through New Orleans. The prince had hoped to keep the Germans close together, perhaps to form an independent German state. His successor, Baron Otfried Hans von Meusebach, dis-

Some of the early German settlers of New Braunfels, Texas, posed for a group portrait in front of the first building put up in their community.
(Library of Congress)

agreed. John O. Meusebach—as he preferred to be known in democratic America—believed that the Germans should settle among other immigrants. So the Germans formed many settlements scattered around Texas, mainly along the coast and up into the south-central region. In the end the *Adelsverein* corporation—meant to make a profit—went bankrupt. But large numbers of Germans continued to make their way to Texas. In 1854, the population of Galveston was about one-third German.

Texas had entirely different soil and climate than Germany. Stillthe German immigrants were generally successful. Texan H.H. McConnell, writing in 1889, commented about the German settlements around New Braunfels: "This whole region . . . is settled very largely by old country Germans, and they have left their impress of industry, order and economy on this section, as they have always done wherever they have found a home in the new world."

Like other German-Americans, they mostly worked the farms themselves, along with hired hands. Other Texans, who relied heavily on slaves, sometimes angrily called the Germans "damned Dutch abolitionists."

To the Heartland

But most German immigrants did not join colonies. Like most German-American pioneers, they usually moved westward singly or with their families. By the late 1840s these new immigrants were moving in large numbers into the Midwest, especially into Illinois, Iowa, and Wisconsin. There many helped open up to cultivation the prime farmlands of America's Midwest.

Many other German immigrants settled in the young and growing cities of the Midwest—cities like Chicago, Milwaukee, Des Moines, Davenport, Dubuque, and Sheboygan. In 1850 Milwaukee had a large enough German community—perhaps 40 percent of the population—to proclaim itself a "German Athens." German immigrants were beginning to found the breweries for which Milwaukee later became famous.

As in the past, most of these German immigrants were Protestants, especially Lutherans. But among these were a significant number of Jews and Catholics. German Jews established themselves in—and made substantial contributions to—most of the cities with substantial German populations. A large number of German Catholics congregated in

Wisconsin—so many, in fact, that a Catholic archdiocese was created there in the 1840s, led by German-Swiss bishop (later archbishop) John Martin Henni.

Becoming Americans

In the young Midwest, German immigrants generally settled among other Americans—and other new immigrants. As they joined with others in local government, schools, churches, and social organizations, they gradually—if not in the first generation, then in the next—dropped their German language and adopted English for both private and public use. With this momentous change, they were well on their way to becoming not German-Americans, but simply Americans. In fact, many German visitors to America in the mid-19th century complained about how quickly German immigrants shed their old culture for the new.

The western settlements tended to break down religious barriers, too, starting with the early settlements in Kentucky and Ohio. Frontier folk at first had few churches or ministers, so traveling preachers would "ride a circuit," preaching to each settlement in turn. Local people—immigrants of varying religious and ethnic backgrounds—would often meet in a cabin or barn to hear the preacher. The old arguments—between "old" and "new" Lutherans, for example—seemed less important to many people on the frontier. Since frontier life was lonely, these religious gatherings were also social events. The great religious "camp meetings" so common in the late 19th and early 20th-century Midwest probably sprang from these early frontier meetings.

The religious organizations in the East Coast states tried to exercise some control over the frontier churches. The Lutheran churches of Tennessee were under the direction of the Lutheran synod of North Carolina until 1820, for example. Those in Ohio were at first under Pennsylvania. But gradually churches in the pioneer regions developed their own synods. On the frontier, German Protestants grew to be more and more like the mainstream American Protestants. In the mid-19th century, when large numbers of Lutherans arrived fresh from Germany, they were horrified at the way the German-Americans had (as they saw it) drifted away from "proper" Lutheranism. Not all Germans merged into the religious mainstream, of course. But the trend was for them to resolve religious differences.

Germans in the Cities

In the 1830s and 1840s, while new German immigrants were opening up lands of the Midwest, many others were settling in the cities along the East Coast. By 1850, New York City alone probably had over 100,000 German-Americans.

Like many other ethnic groups, German-Americans set up organizations to help new immigrants adjust to life in America. The *Deutsche Gesellschaft* (German Society), for example, operated to help newcomers in New York City from at least 1784. Prominent German-Americans—such as Revolutionary War General Friedrich von Steuben and millionaire fur trader John Jacob Astor—served as officers and supporters of such groups. Philadelphia baker Christopher Ludwig, too, left part of his more modest estate to the *Deutsche Gesellschaft* on his death.

Many of these urban immigrants were highly literate people. They founded newspapers, publishing houses, and bookstores in many Eastern cities. These offered German-language publications to German-Americans, new and old. In 1848 approximately 70 German-language newspapers were published in the United States, half of them in Pennsylvania. Among the finest was Philadelphia's *Alte und Neue Welt* ("Old and New World"), founded by Johann George Wesselhöft after his arrival—with his own hand press—in 1833. New York had four German-language papers, including the *New Yorker Staatszeitung*, founded in late 1834 by Oswald Ottendorfer. Almost all the major centers of German settlement had their own German-language press, including Baltimore, Cincinnati, St. Louis, Milwaukee, Galveston, New Orleans, and Charleston. So did many smaller cities, such as Canton, Ohio, and Reading, Pennsylvania.

These newspapers helped keep strong the German immigrants' ties with each other and with their heritage. Their culture formed a large part of the coverage. The papers also kept the new immigrants well informed about political affairs in America, as well as in Germany. All the great social issues of the day were discussed in these papers, including slavery and political corruption. So these newspapers helped many immigrants learn about their new country. The result was that, although the newspapers were in German, they sped the movement of new German immigrants into the mainstream of American life.

Among the immigrants of the 1830s and 1840s were a number of distinguished thinkers and teachers. Scholars from Germany's fine universities brought their learning to American universities. Several became professors at Harvard University, where some of them worked closely with and influenced many of New England's leading scholars and artists. They also translated into English works from major German writers, such as Goethe and Schiller.

They had other influences as well. Carl Follen introduced physical education to Harvard, became a Unitarian minister, and worked for the abolition of slavery. Francis Lieber taught political economy, history, swimming, and physical education at universities in Boston, New York, and South Carolina. Sometimes called the "Father of Political Science," Lieber wrote the important works *Political Ethics* and *Civil Liberty and Self-Government*. Franz Joseph Grund, a German from Bohemia, wrote biographies for the two major political parties of the time, the Democrats and the Whigs, and was later a consul in the diplomatic service.

Among the liberal German immigrants were several notable political leaders. Gustav Körner, for example, had led unsuccessful revolts in Munich and Frankfurt. Jailed for the first, he fled after the second to the United States in 1833. Starting out as a "Latin farmer" in Belleville, Illinois, Körner became active in politics. At first a Democrat and a judge on the Illinois Supreme Court in 1845, he later helped build the new Republican Party and served as Lieutenant Governor of Illinois. In 1862 he became the United States Minister to Spain. His fellow liberal George Bunsen became superintendent of schools in Belleville, introducing some modern German methods of instruction.

Not all liberal German immigrants achieved such success, and so quickly. Some university-educated scholars worked as unskilled day laborers, building canals in Pennsylvania and elsewhere, and some tried farming, only to fail miserably. But most eventually found themselves in communities where their education and skills made real contributions.

By 1850, people of German background already made up a quarter of the United States population. Within a decade that would rise to 30 percent. The German-language press kept alive many new immigrants' interest in their heritage, but many learned English quickly and became influential figures in the young and growing America. Surprisingly, this would bring them into conflict with many in the next and largest wave of German immigrants.

7

The Main Wave

. . . we as Germans are not called upon here to form a separate nationality but rather to contribute to the American nationality the strongest there is in us . . .

> *Carl Schurz, German immigrant,*
> *Civil War general, Missouri*
> *Senator, Secretary of the Interior*

The 1850s saw the start of a much larger and different German immigration. The most significant of the new immigrants was a group of political refugees, called the Forty-Eighters, who came to America after the failure of Germany's 1848 revolutions.

The Grays and the Greens

The Forty-Eighters who began arriving in America in 1850 were a mixed lot. Some, as in all revolutions, were waiting for a time when they could return to a free, democratic Germany. Some hoped to found a separate German republic in America. Others threw in their lot wholeheartedly with their new country.

Most were shocked at the America they found. It certainly was a working democracy and a united nation, as Germany was not. But the reality of the rough, new country—the dirt and poverty, the crime and corruption, the slavery, the obsession with wealth, the ignorance and apathy—was very far from the America of their dreams.

Seeing these problems, many Forty-Eighters were impatient. They wanted to remake the world, starting with the United States. They saw themselves as "Greens"—full of spirit and ready for action. And they saw earlier German-Americans as "Grays"—old, drained, ineffective people.

The Greens criticized the Grays for so quickly giving up their proud German language and culture to become "American barbarians." They even, sometimes, money. As a result, they often had a good deal of in-become an influential politician in America—"the gray Gustav." Young reformers with little experience of practical realities, the Greens thought the Grays should have immediately ended such injustices as slavery and political corruption. Many Greens were also free-thinkers, critical of the many churches in America and the power of the clergy, especially in the Catholic church.

The Grays were naturally bitter about criticisms of their success in America. They thought that the Greens had not taken the trouble to learn about the country they wanted to transform. And many of the Grays were offended at the Greens' scholarly and scientific ideas—representing the new wave in European thinking—which sharply differed from their more conservative religious views.

The result was a sharp split between the Forty-Eighters and many of the earlier German immigrants to America. The split was quickly reflected in a different set of social and cultural organizations—newspapers, social organizations, lecture societies, scholarly groups, and the like. Many of these Forty-Eighters had a great deal of intelligence, talent, culture, and even, sometimes money. As a result, they often had a good deal of in-fluence—far greater than their numbers, which were at most several thousand, would suggest.

The Forty-Eighters

Many Forty-Eighters were scholars and writers. They thought the old German-language newspapers dull and badly written, so they founded many new ones, from large daily German-American papers to short-lived radical sheets. Many Forty-Eighters wrote for German-language papers while pursuing other careers, as in law, medicine, or politics. For example, Carl Schurz, later a senator and cabinet minister and perhaps the greatest of all the Forty-Eighters, began his career in America as an editor on a German-language paper.

The Forty-Eighters also wrote many other types of works as well. Within and outside universities, they produced scholarly works, histories, philosophies, poetry, literary journals, reviews, and novels, including some in German about immigrant life in America. So many Forty-

Eighters were writers that German-Americans formed their own national literary association, in addition to smaller interest groups.

The Forty-Eighters were appalled at the low level of education in America—the untrained teachers, the poor textbooks, the rough school buildings, the limited number of subjects, and the ignorance of new educational ideas from Europe. They set about to change all that. All over the country they founded private schools for German-American students, and served as teachers and principals. Their hopes were to preserve German culture and to serve as a model for local public schools. They also founded training schools, like the German-American Teachers Seminary in Milwaukee and the German and English Institute in Baltimore, to set high standards of education. Leading German-American educators like Karl Douai, Marie Kraus-Bolte, and Margaretha Meyer (who later married Carl Schurz) introduced the German kindergarten to America.

Forty-Eighters made major contributions in medicine. In the mid-19th century, American pharmacists had no formal training; physicians and surgeons had only a year or two of medical education. By contrast, German pharmacists and doctors had both university and graduate training. Those who arrived as Forty-Eighters immediately raised the level of medical treatment wherever they settled. Even more important, they pushed for more and better training for all medical people.

Many of these medically trained immigrants had strong social views as well. Imprisoned in Germany for five years after 1848, in America Abraham Jacobi founded the German Dispensary in New York in 1857, to provide medication to poor German immigrants. Later he founded the German Hospital (now Lenox Hill Hospital) and a nursing school. As a professor at New York Medical College, his emphasis on medical care for children earned him the nickname "Father of American Pediatrics." In his eighties, Jacobi served as president of the American Medical Association.

Among the Forty-Eighters were some early and active supporters of women's liberation. Mathilde Franziska Anneke published a Milwaukee paper in the 1850s, *Deutsche Frauen-Zeitung*, and later was a powerful speaker on women's rights in the East. Some male Forty-Eighters and Turner organizations also supported women's right to vote.

Forty-Eighters also made major contributions to agriculture in America. They introduced new plants to several parts of the country, notably California, and began farm-scale cultivation of fruits and trees before found only in small gardens. German-American agricultural scientists taught in universities and did research aimed at making farming more

Forty-Eighter Abraham Jacobi was called the "Father of American Pediatrics" for his work in providing medical help for the poor, especially children.
(Library of Congress)

scientific. Internationally known German-American Professor Eugene W. Hilgard, for example, taught at the universities of Michigan, Mississippi, and California, and also advised government agencies.

Forty-Eighters helped establish the wine industry of northern California. Former Heidelberg law student Julius Dresel planted vineyards in California's Sonoma County in 1858. German-born Charles Krug, who had gone back to Germany for the 1848 revolutions and returned to America after their failure, founded a vineyard and winery in the Napa Valley in 1860. When the grapevines of Europe were being killed off by a terrible disease, German-American plant scientists from St. Louis discovered how to graft the European vine onto a disease-resistant American one, saving the European wine industry.

New German immigrants helped the early brewery industry expand even further, especially in and around Milwaukee. The Pabst Brewing Company was founded in 1844 by Jacob Best and his sons. Five years later Austrian immigrant August Krug began brewing beer for his wife Anna's restaurant, founding the Joseph Schlitz Brewing Company. In 1855 Frederick Miller, former brewmaster at Hohenzollern Castle in Germany, bought a small brewery outside Milwaukee, founding today's massive Miller Brewing Company. German brewers worked elsewhere,

From massive factories to small private breweries, Germans and German-Americans have long been linked with fine beer. (Harper's, late 19th century)

too. Eberhard Anheuser, a St. Louis brewer since 1852, was later joined by his Bavarian son-in-law, Adolphus Busch, forming the Bavarian Brewing Company, later Anheuser-Busch, makers of Budweiser beer.

Other Newcomers

In addition to the Forty-Eighters, the 1850s saw the arrival of tens of thousands of ordinary Germans—farmers, artisans, small-business owners, and the like. These newcomers generally followed the pattern of settlement set by earlier German immigrants. Some settled in the old cities of the East Coast or the new cities of the Midwest. Others followed the main pathways west to the farmlands in the heart of the country.

Many new immigrants continued to come as families or in groups. But increasingly, as shipping schedules became more regular, individuals, generally young men, came on their own. Most were Protestants from the Lutheran or Reformed churches. Few in this period were sectarians, but many were Jewish or Catholic.

From the 1840s on, large numbers of German Jews came to America. Some who were Forty-Eighters came as professionals or artists. But many others started in America as poor peddlers, setting up tent-like shops or stands on city streets or traveling about the countryside selling their wares. Some remained peddlers or small shopkeepers, but others became quite prosperous. Once they earned enough money, they would establish regular stores around the country. Or, if they earned or gathered together enough money, they started banks or manufacturing businesses, notably in the garment industry.

The Seligman brothers, for example, started out as peddlers in Pennsylvania and then founded a store in Lancaster, while other relatives became peddlers in the South. Later they settled in New York, operating various banking and manufacturing firms. When the Civil War arrived, the Seligmans were awarded the contract to supply uniforms for the Union army. They were paid, not in cash but in American bonds, which they had to sell in European markets—not an easy thing, when the country was at war.

Like other German immigrants, many of these Jews were proud of their German heritage. They often kept German as their main language at home. Some prosperous German Jews, like some German Protestants, even sent their children back to Germany for at least part of their education.

Many of these German Jews carried with them ideas of the German reform movements—not only political, but also religious. In America, some of them, led especially by Rabbi Isaac Meyer Wise of Cincinnati, Ohio, formed a new wing of their religion, called Reform Judaism, which they felt was better suited to modern, democratic America.

Smaller numbers of German Catholics arrived in this period, also. They tended to congregate in places, such as Wisconsin, that had German-speaking priests. German Catholics bitterly resented Irish priests who criticized them as "anti-American" for wanting to keep their own language and customs. German and Irish Catholics would struggle for power within the American Catholic church for many decades. In the long run, the Irish came to dominate, even though German Catholics were later joined by many other Catholics from Central and Southern Europe.

Know-Nothings

The mid-19th century was a period of massive emigration not only from Germany but also from other parts of Europe as well, notably from

Ireland and Scandinavia. These new immigrants met a very special situation in America. Anglo-Americans—those of British descent—were questioning unlimited immigration into their country. They feared that the large numbers of immigrants would change the nature of the country, that Europeans would take away "American" jobs, that the newcomers were criminals and bums, and so on. The people who held strongly to such fears and prejudices were generally called Nativists or Know-Nothings.

From then to now, every major immigrant group has had to face such prejudices. And from then to now, every new immigrant group has proven such fears to be wrong—and has not only entered the mainstream of American life but contributed greatly to it. But in the 1850s Know-Nothing feelings ran very high among many Anglo-Americans. They were especially unhappy with those people who refused to give up their language and enter fully into the English-speaking American culture.

Some German-Americans thought that the various immigrant groups ought to unite against the Know-Nothing Anglo-Americans. But many Forty-Eighters strongly opposed that idea, largely because of some prejudices of their own, as this sharply worded excerpt from the 1854 *Wisconsin Demokrat* reveals:

The idea of forming a union of foreigners against Nativism is wholly wrong, and destroys the possibility of any influence on

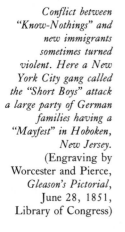

Conflict between "Know-Nothings" and new immigrants sometimes turned violent. Here a New York City gang called the "Short Boys" attack a large party of German families having a "Mayfest" in Hoboken, New Jersey. (Engraving by Worcester and Pierce, Gleason's Pictorial, June 28, 1851, Library of Congress)

our part; it would drive us into a union with Irishmen . . . In our struggle we are not concerned with nationality, but with principles; we are for liberty, and against union with Irishmen who stand nearer barbarism and brutality than civilization and humanity. The Irish are our natural enemies, not because they are Irishmen but because they are the truest guards of Popery.

Such views naturally drove wedges between German-Americans of different religions—Catholics, Jews, and the many Protestant churches and sects.

The Civil War

On the eve of the Civil War German-Americans were generally troubled and divided. Many German-Americans were politically active, but they were often pulled in different directions. Some, especially Forty-Eighters, still hoped to found a German state. They held many political conventions to that end from the 1830s to the early 1860s, in Pittsburgh, Louisville, Chicago, Cleveland, and several times in Missouri.

Many German-Americans became active in the new anti-slavery Republican party. They strongly supported the Republican presidential candidate in 1860, Abraham Lincoln, and often accompanied him on his campaign tours. In a letter home, Lincoln wrote: "The old Pennsylvania Dutch follow me like children, although they can only half understand me. The Democrats are furious, and wherever I have spoken they telegraph like mad in all directions for German speakers to neutralize my speeches."

Many other German-Americans were Democrats and remained so, though less often in areas where the Democrats were strongly associated with Know-Nothing attitudes. Still, when Lincoln was elected, many German-Americans were proud of the role they played in helping him to gain the presidency.

With the coming of the Civil War, less urgent political arguments mostly gave way before the massive split between North and South. The overwhelming majority of German-Americans took the side of the North, for a variety of reasons.

Many German-Americans simply believed slavery was wrong. The anti-slavery stance of German-Americans went back to Pastorius and the early German Quakers. But not all German-Americans were against slavery. The Old Lutherans of Missouri, for example, thought the Bible justified it. And some German-Americans, especially in the South, did hold slaves. But most opposed slavery as being against their religion and against liberty.

Many German-Americans supported the North because they believed the breakup of the American Union would be disastrous. They had, after all, come from a land too-long divided into petty states, and suffering because of it. To them, union was the ideal.

German-Americans tended to favor the North partly because most of them had settled there. But even in the North, support for the Union cause was not automatic. German-Americans, especially conservative Catholics, in some parts of Wisconsin, for example, remained strongly behind the antiwar Democratic party, right through the Civil War. At the other extreme, some radical German-Americans were angered that Lincoln did not move faster to end the war and slavery.

Fewer German-Americans had settled in the South—perhaps 70,000 at the beginning of the Civil War—and they reflected a wider range of opinion. Many German-Americans in Southern states voted against secession. When that vote failed, some fled north, especially to West Virginia and to Union-held Alexandria, Virginia. From Texas some fled to Missouri or Mexico. Quite apart from their feelings about slavery, many German-Americans did not want to break their oath of allegiance to the United States. A German-American group in Texas, led by doctor-soldier Anthony Dignowitz, even hoped to have Texas withdraw from the Confederacy and ally itself with the Union army. On the other hand, some German-Americans supported secession, even some who opposed slavery. After August 1861, Confederate law required citizens to take an oath supporting the secession, or face possible expulsion. Those who did not take the oath became, at least, suspect. Some heavily German antisecession areas of Texas, for example, were occupied by Confederate troops. Anti-draft riots were held in several cities, such as Fredericksburg, Texas, where about 25 German-Americans were court-martialed and executed.

In border states such as Maryland, Kentucky, and Missouri, German-Americans did much to tip the balance toward the North and away from the South. As President Theodore Roosevelt said in a 1903 speech:

> It would have been out of the question to have kept Missouri
> loyal [to the Union] had it not been for the German element

therein. So it was in Kentucky—and but little less important was the part played by the Germans in Maryland.

Sometimes—as in Maryland—this was largely a matter of influence and ideas. Sometimes, as in Missouri, it was also a matter of action.

Much of Missouri was pro-Confederacy, including its governor. He had planned to take the heavily stocked U.S. arsenal at St. Louis for the Confederates, which would ensure that the South held the lower Mississippi Valley. But he reckoned without the anti-slavery German-American Turner societies. Pro-Union Germans drove a brewery wagon into the arsenal and replaced their beer barrels with arms and ammunition. In the end, German-Americans, many of them students, kept the arsenal from falling into Confederate hands.

As in the Revolutionary War, many German-Americans initially hoped to remain neutral and not be forced to take sides. Religious pacifists were exempted from military service, though many in the mid-Atlantic states lived in a battleground. But when forced to choose, most German-Americans chose Lincoln and the Union.

The Soldiers

German-Americans were among the first to enlist when Lincoln called for volunteers, often forming all-German-speaking regiments, like the Steuben Regiment, from states such as New York, Pennsylvania, Ohio, Indiana, Illinois, and Wisconsin. Many of these regiments were formed by Turner societies enlisting as a group.

Many new German immigrants also joined the army on arrival. Some were recruited in Europe by Union agents, with promises of citizenship at the end of the war and free land in the Western states, under the Homestead Act. Among these recruits were many German military officers, whose skills were useful in the fighting. Recruiting agents also met incoming ships, offering young male immigrants bonuses for joining the Union army.

In all, about 176,000 German-born soldiers, and as many as 500,000 or 600,000 Americans of German descent, served in the Union Army of about 2,000,000. Confederate General Robert E. Lee reportedly said: "Take the Dutch [Germans] out of the Union army and we could whip the Yankees easily."

In the Confederate army, too, Germans formed some all- or mostly German units, often commanded by German officers, from states like Louisiana, Georgia, Virginia, and Texas. A Prussian officer, Baron Heros von Borcke, ran the Union blockade to join the Confederate army and became Inspector General of J.E.B. Stuart's cavalry troops. German-born Karl Gustav Memminger, brought to Charleston as a child, served as Secretary of the Treasury for the Confederacy. Charleston's Fort Wagener was named for a German-American colonel of the Confederate artillery.

Sometimes Germans fought each other in battle. Several reports tell of opposing German units singing German songs across the lines. In West Virginia's Kanawha Valley, we are told:

> . . . when the firing was over, as night came on, nothing was to be heard but the roaring of the waters, intermingled now and then with snatches of song from some of the German soldiers on either side, which produced a touching effect at such an hour. Ofttimes one of our Germans could be seen leaning on his rifle, listening to the sounds of his mother tongue as they were wafted over from the enemy's camp. At times, one of the sentinels would shout across—"From what part do you come, countryman? I am a Bavarian."

Some Northerners questioned the German contribution to the war, charging that their numbers were inflated and that they were not good soldiers. Others charged that the Union army was an "overseas orphanage for cracked up German officers." Certainly German soldiers shared in defeats as well as victories. But these criticisms probably sprang largely from Know-Nothing feelings. In truth, many Germans and German-Americans served with distinction, not only in the rank and file but also in the officer corps. Among the many German-born Union officers were some with military experience, including General Franz Sigel, who helped hold Missouri for the Union, and Forty-Eighter General August von Willich, who fought at Shiloh. Some others, like General Carl Schurz, had little military background, but were natural leaders. Many officers of German background but American birth also served, including General William Rosencrans, General Herman Haupt, and the young George Armstrong Custer, later famous as an Indian fighter in the West.

Germans also contributed scientific and technical skills. German doctors and surgeons served the Union forces, including Dr. Gustav Weber and Viennese-trained Julius von Hausesn. Count Zeppelin,

Major General Franz Sigel, who helped hold Missouri for the Union, was but one of many Union officers of German background in the Civil War. (Library of Congress)

famous for developing lighter-than-air flying craft, served in the Union cavalry as officer and engineer.

After the War

German-Americans were proud of their part in the Civil War. Having fought side by side with other Americans, they came to better appreciate the wonderful variety of American peoples and culture. And people of other backgrounds came to better understand and respect them. As a result, many more German-Americans moved into the mainstream. The Know-Nothings did not simply disappear—their sentiments are with us still. But their prejudice toward the Germans was decreased.

Perhaps no one illustrated this German-American move into the mainstream better than Carl Schurz. A Forty-Eighter, he had arrived in America in 1852 as a 23-year-old university student. While working as a journalist, he became active in the anti-slavery movement, especially in the Republican Party, and a friend of Abraham Lincoln. After serving as a general in the Civil War, he was a popular and influential senator from Missouri. Then in 1877, only 25 years after coming to America,

President Rutherford Hayes appointed him Secretary of the Interior. There he introduced new European ideas on the management of forest resources. He also addressed with thoughtfulness special American problems, among them the need for conservation, the establishment of a national park service, civil service reform, and the problems of Native Americans being pressed by settlers moving west. Later in his life, Schurz returned to journalism as editor of the influential publications. *The Nation* and *Harper's Weekly*. On his death in 1906, no less a figure than Mark Twain wrote a tribute, calling Schurz a friend and a "master in citizenship."

Carl Schurz was an inspiration to many German-Americans. By his example and advice, he urged them to give up the idea of separate German states or communities, and to become fully American. Many followed his example, especially those who were already in the United States by the end of the Civil War.

But many others held fast to their German identity—among them large numbers of new German immigrants who arrived after the Civil War. Many of these new German immigrants were drawn to the open lands beyond the Mississippi River. There they moved to settle the last American frontier.

The New Frontier

The United States was expanding toward the Pacific Ocean. This move had, in fact, begun well before the Civil War. From the 1820s Americans—among them German-Americans—had been trading from the Mississippi River towns across the Great Plains to places like Santa Fe in New Mexico and San Antonio in Texas. These territories were then part of Mexico, but after the Mexican-American War of 1848, they became part of the Union.

Other Americans had been exploring the mountain trails to Oregon and the Northwest. Among them were fur traders employed by John Jacob Astor. This immigrant, son of a German butcher, became a multi-millionaire through the fur trade, and his riches later built the famous New York hotel, the Waldorf-Astoria.

Americans had also been trading by sea with California for many decades, sailing all the way around the tip of South America to do so. Few took the long, hard overland trip. But in 1848 gold was discovered in California near a mill owned by a Swiss-German immigrant, John A.

Sutter. By 1849, people were streaming across the plains to join the Gold Rush to California. Among them were many German-Americans and German immigrants direct from Europe, drawn by the prospect of gold. Within a year, the United States had annexed California as well.

Having staked their claim to the lands all the way to the Pacific, the Americans set about peopling the vast territory. German-Americans from east of the Mississippi joined other Americans streaming to the Great Plains. Following the standard immigrant pattern, these "old hands" would leave for the frontier. After the Civil War, many settled on free land under the Homestead Act. Once established in a new community, they would be followed by friends and family from their earlier American homes and also by chains of immigrants fresh from Europe, drawn by America letters. German immigrants had especially close ties with—and often settled alongside—Scandinavian immigrants, notably Swedes, Norwegians, Danes, and Icelanders.

Germans from Russia

It was in this period that Russian-Germans came to America seeking new homes. In 1872, some small scouting parties from the German Black Sea colonies selected settlement sites in Nebraska and the Dakota Territory. Larger groups of Russian-German settlers began arriving in these areas in mid-1873. Others followed later, including some Hutterite and Mennonite groups, and some from the Volga River colonies. They spread throughout the region—into the Dakotas, Nebraska, Kansas, Minnesota, and Colorado, and later into Idaho and Montana—and also into the western prairies of Canada. Some Russian-German Mennonites even settled as far west as the San Joaquin Valley of California.

Most of the Russian-Germans from the Black Sea area set up separate communities in America, trying—as they had in Russia—to keep their own German language and culture. While most Russian-Germans stayed on the farm, some of the Volga immigrants gave up the idea of separate German colonies and instead moved into the Midwestern cities.

Prairie Country

Life on the plains was hard. Like the earliest German settlers back in the 17th century, the prairie pioneers often survived the first year or few living in an earthen cave-cabin, covered with great slabs of sod cut from the prairie. Only after the soil started to yield crops were there time and money to build a log cabin. Plagues of grasshoppers and other pests could wipe out much of a year's crop—as happened to some of the earliest Russian-German settlers in their first three years.

In the 1870s some whole countries were settled mostly by Germans. In such areas, German often remained the language of both farm and town for decades, sometimes continuing into the 1930s. The new settlers had their own German newspapers. The Russian-Germans in the Dakota town of Yankton, for example, had the *Dakota Freie Presse*, founded in 1874. And, as in most new immigrant communities, the church remained at the center of not only religious but also social life. A number of German Catholics congregated in Minnesota, attracted by a missionary priest.

By the late 19th century Germans had settled throughout the states of the upper Midwest, most heavily in Wisconsin. Large numbers were also found in Minnesota, Illinois, and Ohio. The other main area of German settlement was in the mid-Atlantic states. New York State claimed the most German immigrants—perhaps three out of every ten after 1850. Fewer German immigrants settled in the South, New England, the Rocky Mountain states, and the Pacific Coast.

German settlers played an enormous role in opening up the vast ranges of the northern Great Plains. In 1900, German farmers—people born in Germany or with at least one parent born there—owned more than half a million farms in the United States, three times as many as any other ethnic group. Many more farms were in the hands of American-born farmers of German descent. The production of American farmlands—a wonder of the world—owes more than a little to the skill, intelligence, and scientific methods of these hard-working farmers. Though few Germans were ranchers, the Kleberg family used scientific crossbreeding of cattle to help build America's largest ranch, the 1,125,000-acre King Ranch in Texas.

In the Cities

But while German farmers were opening up the prairies, more and more German immigrants were heading for the cities. By 1890, four out of every ten new German immigrants settled in a city of over 25,000 people. In 1900, New York City alone had well over 300,000 German-born residents—not counting the many other New Yorkers of German descent, and the many other German immigrants who lived across the

Hudson River in New Jersey. New York had so many because it was the main entry port, and a booming city with jobs for many. At the same time, Chicago—the hub of the upper Midwest—had over 200,000 German-born immigrants. Many other cities had over 30,000 German-born immigrants, including Philadelphia with over 73,000 and, in descending order, Milwaukee, St. Louis, Buffalo, Cleveland, Detroit, Cincinnati, Pittsburgh, San Francisco, and Baltimore.

In many cities, Germans settled in distinct sections—often called something like "Little Germany," "Germantown," or (as in Cleveland) "Over the Rhine." There, German was spoken in the homes, on the streets, and in the shops, and the stores, churches, and social organizations reflected German traditions. A Danish visitor to Milwaukee noted in the 1850s that "many Germans live here who never learn English, and seldom go beyond the German town." That would be true at least through the end of the century, because new immigrants kept flowing in.

Meanwhile, as older immigrants and especially their children began to prosper and adopt American ways, they would often move to other areas, including the suburbs, that were not distinctly ethnic. Around the turn of the century, as German immigration slowed, their old sections would become home to newer immigrant groups.

In the years after the Civil War, fewer German immigrants were farmers and more were skilled artisans. Often they had learned traditional crafts in Germany, working as carpenters, cabinetmakers, tailors, and the like. Many worked with food or drink as bakers, butchers, brewers, distillers, or dairy owners. Others owned stores, taverns, hotels, or restaurants. A fair number worked in the arts, especially in music. Fewer in this period were intellectuals or professionals such as doctors, lawyers, or professors.

By late in the 19th century many German immigrants, nearly one out of every two, were general laborers, with few or no skills, or domestic servants. Among them were many women, who often worked in service occupations as cleaners, waitresses, barmaids, cooks, or nurses. By the turn of the 20th century, many more immigrants were factory workers, drawn by the rapidly growing American industries.

Everyday Life

In the late 19th and early 20th centuries, German-Americans made many contributions to everyday American life. Perhaps most striking is the Christmas tree. Tradition has it that the first Christmas tree in America was one decorated by Hessian soldiers during the Revolutionary War. But the Christmas tree only came to be widely used in Germany in the early 19th century—and new immigrants brought the idea to America. In the late 19th century German-Americans also made popular the practices of sending Christmas cards, often cards produced by German printers in America or abroad, and displaying a Christmas wreath. German-Americans had long since helped spread in America the hymn singing and festive cooking associated with Christmas.

The popular Easter rabbit and brightly colored Easter eggs were also brought to America by the Germans. According to a very old German legend, a goddess named Ostara changed a bird into a rabbit, which would lay eggs on Ostara's birthday. When the Germans adopted Christianity long ago, Ostara became associated with Easter. So, through the old German practices, the rabbit and the painted eggs came to be part of the American Easter.

Germans brought many foods to America, especially sausages of all kinds. But none has reached the popularity of the frankfurter sausage, from Frankfurt, Germany. At some point (some say in St. Louis in the 1880s, others say at New York's Coney Island amusement park in the 1890s) a German immigrant placed the frankfurter on a roll—and an American tradition was born. Much the same took place with the grilled chopped steak brought to America by Germans from Hamburg, probably in the 1880s. At the 1904 St. Louis Exposition, the story goes, a food vendor ran out of plates and instead served the beef on a roll—and soon everyone wanted the new "hamburger."

Many German-Americans turned food into big business. In the 1870s Henry John Heinz started making the high-quality ketchups, relishes, sauces, and other foods that gave his firm the slogan "57 varieties." Milton Hershey, descendant of early Pennsylvania Mennonites, went into the candy business as a teenager in 1876 and struck it rich with the Hershey bar in 1895. Austrian-born Leo Hirschfield created the Tootsie Roll in 1896. Starting in 1869 German-born Henry Heide built a successful family business making such jellied candies as Jujyfruits and JuJubes. In the 1890s German immigrant F.W. Rueckheim wowed Chicago with his candied popcorn called Crackerjacks. German immigrant Dr. Ludwig Roselius created Sanka decaffeinated coffee in the early 1900s. German immigrant brothers Gilbert and Louis Hueblein began to sell pre-mixed cocktails in 1892. In 1912 German immigrant Richard Hellmann began selling the mayonnaise that bears his name from his family's delicatessen. And in delicatessens and German taverns called Rathskellers all over the country, Americans came to know and love German foods such as sauerkraut, liverwurst, pumpernickel bread, pretzels, and, of course, beers and sausages of all kinds.

Business and Industry

Germans also made major contributions in business and industry. Charles Goodnight, descendant of a Virginia German family, invented the chuck wagon, at which food was prepared for cowboys on long-distance cattle drives. Two German brothers, Henry and Clement Studebaker, manufactured the first commercial chuck wagons, started in 1852, and later branched out to make all sorts of horse-drawn wagons and, between 1902 and 1966, a major line of automobiles as well. German-Dutch-American Walter Chrysler headed General Motors, retired, and in 1925 founded the Chrysler Motor Company. German-American Jack Mack built trucks, and the German-born Duesenberg brothers, Fred and August, built luxury racing cars. German-American Frank Seiberling founded the Goodyear Tire Company, making Akron, Ohio, the "Rubber Capital of the World." Harvey Firestone, whose ancestors came from the Alsace and Austria, founded his own tire company in Ohio.

Starting in the 1850s, German-American Isaac Merritt Singer mass-produced sewing machines, making them a household fixture. German-Dutch-American George Westinghouse introduced a series of inventions that formed the core of the Westinghouse Electric Company. German immigrants Jacob J. Bausch and Henry Lomb began making their famous optical lenses in the mid-19th century. German immigrant Ottmar Mergenthaler in 1872 developed the Linotype machine, which revolutionized typesetting. Austrian immigrant John Michael Kohler founded the plumbing fixtures firm that still bears his name. Friedrich Weyerhauser built up a massive timber empire.

John Augustus Roebling came to America and began building bridges in the mid-19th century, spanning the Niagara Falls Whirlpools in 1855 and the Ohio River in Cincinnati in 1866. His most famous work was the Brooklyn Bridge, on which he lost his life in 1869. (It was completed by his son.) Roebling's major innovation was the suspension bridge, a roadway suspended from great wire ropes.

Charles Steinmetz (born Karl August Rudolf Steinmetz) was forced to leave Germany in 1888 for his socialist views. He was an electrical engineering genius, called the "wizard of Schenectady" for his work at General Electric. He made major contributions, little understood by non-scientists. He was once, we are told, called in by Henry Ford to examine a problem generator. Steinmetz looked and listened, made a chalk mark on the generator, and said to cut exactly 16 coils off a cable at that spot. He then presented a bill for $10,000. When Ford asked for a breakdown, Steinmetz replied: "Making chalk mark on generator $1. Knowing where to make chalk mark $9,999."

German-born Moritz Behrend manufactured a line of high-quality business stationery under the name Hammermill. German-American William Mathias Scholl created a million-dollar business of shoes and other footwear under the name Dr. Scholl. With his brothers, German-born Frederick August Otto Schwartz opened his famous toy store in mid-century. In the same period, Austrian-born August Brentano opened the bookstore that led to a chain, and German immigrant William Schlemmer joined with Alfred Hammacher in a hardware store that led to today's one-of-a-kind gadget store.

Often, German-American businesses revolved around music. German-born Heinrich Engelhard Steinweg followed his Forty-Eighter son to America in the 1850s. The family built the still-famous Steinway piano company. Christian Frederick Martin came to America in 1833 and began making the fine guitars that his descendants still craft today. And Rudolph Wurlitzer founded his musical instrument company after coming to Cincinnati in 1856. In the 20th century the Wurlitzer name would be most linked with electronic organs and pianos, and with the massive Radio City Music Hall organ.

Cultural and Social Life

Religion—whether mainline Protestant, sectarian, Catholic, or Jewish—continued to play an important role in the lives of many Germans in America, especially in rural areas. But in the late 19th century, non-religious organizations became more and more central, especially in the cities and towns. Some clubs were purely social, such as coffee circles and singing societies. Some served practical purposes, such as volunteer fire companies or local militias. Some served economic needs, as did mutual

The German-American firm of Steinway & Sons in New York City employed hundreds of skilled craftsmen, many of them German immigrants, to build their famous pianos. (Frank Leslie's, May 28, 1864)

benefit societies that provided Germans with life insurance and loans. Some were ethnic brotherhoods, such as the Sons of Herrmann, founded in 1840. Many groups combined several motives, such as the German-speaking lodges of such fraternal organizations (brotherhoods) as the Masons or the Odd Fellows, where members made useful business and social connections. Many organizations met in German taverns, which also hosted a wide array private feasts, celebrations, and family parties, generally accompanied by singing and dancing.

In most cities with large German populations, singing societies were common. From mid-century on, many cities held a singing competition called Sängerfest. In 1900 in Brooklyn alone, 6,000 German-American singers from 174 singing societies competed for honors. Much of the music was classical—oratorios or opera selections were favored—though folk songs were sung, too. Many cities also had amateur drama groups from the 1840s on. Germans also sponsored many musical organizations—symphonies, chamber groups, opera companies, and bands.

Amateur societies laid the basis for professional groups in many cities. Philadelphia German-Americans founded the first symphony orchestra in the country, in 1820. In New York, Leopold and Walter Damrosch, a German father and son from what is now Poland, spurred enormous musical activity. One of many Germans brought in to conduct concerts of New York's Philharmonic Society, Leopold helped found the New York Symphony Society in 1879, and was later succeeded by Walter. They are both honored by New York's Damrosch Park. Other cities also had their orchestral societies, and were visited by touring orchestras. Most of the musicians and conductors for the concerts in this period were Germans, who also staffed the many music schools that sprang up around the country.

Leopold Damrosch and other German-Americans also helped found the Metropolitan Opera Company in New York, adding many German operas and singers to the popular Italian works and performers. Another German immigrant from what is now Poland, Oscar Hammerstein, founded the Manhattan Opera House in New York in 1906, rivaling the Metropolitan until they bought him out in 1910. Among the many German opera stars brought to New York in this period was Czechoslovakian-born Austrian singer Ernestine Schumann-Heink.

In the same way, amateur dramatic societies provided an audience for professional German theatrical companies, which toured the main German-American centers from the 1850s until World War I. Cities like New York, Chicago, Philadelphia, and Milwaukee had separate theaters for plays—classic and new—presented by German-speaking actors. One popular favorite was Schiller's *Wilhelm Tell*. Some of these German

Opera star Ernestine Schumann-Heink was one of the many German-born singers and musicians to enrich the American cultural scene in the late 19th and early 20th centuries.
(Library of Congress)

theaters lasted for decades. The German theater founded in Cincinnati in 1846 by actor Christian Thielmann and his family lasted until 1918. In popular entertainment, too, German-Americans made special contributions. Starting in 1871, the sons of German immigrant harness-maker August Rüngeling began the Ringling Brothers Circus. Traveling around the country giving shows under the "Big Top," the Ringling Brothers Circus gave joy to millions. It later merged with the Barnum & Bailey Circus.

German-Americans also made their mark in the visual arts. In 1852, Emmanuel Leutze painted his famous work, *Washington Crossing the Delaware*, modeling the river after his memories of the Rhine. Berlin-trained Albert Bierstadt was the best known of the many German-American artists who were inspired by the beauty of America. German-American sculptors produced many of the works now displayed in public buildings in Washington, D.C., and other cities around America. German-born William Frismuth designed the top of the Washington Monument.

Art from Germany also was brought to America, sometimes for tours, sometimes to be placed in American museums, such as the Germanic Museum at Harvard University. This was founded in 1903 with money from wealthy German-Americans and gifts also from German nobles and cities.

In a different artistic vein was the work of German-born Thomas Nast. While still a teenager, Nast became an illustrator for the popular magazine *Leslie's Weekly*. His pictures of Civil War battles were world-famous, and Abraham Lincoln commented: "Thomas Nast has been our best recruiting sergeant." Later Nast became a political cartoonist for *Harper's Weekly*, where he created the elephant and donkey symbols that today are "mascots" for the Republican and Democratic parties—and also the popular image of a fat, jolly Santa Claus flying through the sky in a sleigh pulled by reindeer. Starting in 1897, German immigrant Randolph Dirks began drawing America's longest-running comic strip, "The Katzenjammer Kids," based on a similar German strip.

German-Americans had a profound impact on higher education in this country, especially scientific education. In 1876 Johns Hopkins University, modeled on the German university and staffed largely by German professors, was founded in Baltimore. In its stress on a sound basic university education *before* (not instead of) scientific training, Johns Hopkins set the model for modern undergraduate and graduate

This German-American printer, retired from regular work, taught his special art and craft to young schoolchilren. (By Lewis W. Hine, New York Public Library, 1905)

programs. On the university's 25th anniversary, Harvard University's President Eliot applauded Johns Hopkins stating that it had:

> . . . lifted every other university in the country in its departments of arts and sciences . . . the graduate school of Harvard University, started feebly in 1870 and 1871, did not thrive until the example of Johns Hopkins forced our faculty to put their strength into the development of our instruction for graduates. And what was true of Harvard was true of every other university in the land which aspired to create an advanced school of arts and sciences.

German-Americans also led the way in establishing certain kinds of special schools. Prussian-born Bernhard Fernow headed the first school of forestry in America, founded at Cornell in 1898. Others soon followed, at Michigan, Georgia, Yale, and Harvard, all of them staffed largely by German or German-taught professors.

German-Americans also helped found and fund countless other institutions, such as schools, hospitals, museums, old-age homes, and orphanages. Wealthy families like the Astors, the Rockefellers, the Busches, and the Loebs gave huge sums. They and others also provided inspiration. German-American Henry Bergh in 1866 founded the Society for the Prevention of Cruelty to Animals, modeled on a British organization. In 1874, he founded the Society for the Prevention of Cruelty to Children. New York's Legal Aid Society, which gives free legal advice to anyone who needs it, was originally founded as the German Society.

Political Life

Politics and philosophy also drew many Germans into organizations. The Turner organizations, combining athletics and liberal politics, continued to be active after the Civil War—some into the late 20th century. They founded schools for gymnastics teachers, in New York and Milwaukee, and sponsored athletic tournaments. But many other groups were more purely political—debating societies, lecture-and-discussion groups, or special interest groups.

Among these were groups of "free-thinkers," many of them Forty-Eighters. These were anticlerical nonbelievers who grouped themselves into "congregations" aimed at providing rational alternatives to religion. In the 1850s Wisconsin alone had 30 such "free congregations." Many survived into the 20th century. Others merged with Turner or socialist organizations, or joined with independent philosophical groups such as the Unitarians.

German-American workers also formed many political organizations focusing on reform and the rights of labor. Some of these were primarily socialist or communist groups, such as those led by mid-19th century German-American labor leaders Wilhelm Weitling and Joseph Weydemeyer. German-Americans from such groups in 1869 helped form the International Workingmen's Association in America and the later Socialist Labor Party.

Some German-American labor activists were anarchists, who wanted to do away with government altogether. Labor activities sometimes turned violent, as when a bomb was exploded during a demonstration in Chicago's Haymarket Square in 1886, killing eleven people, seven of them policemen. Although no clear evidence linked them with throwing or making the bomb, seven people—five of them German-Americans—were convicted of the bombing. (Four were hanged, and three were later pardoned.)

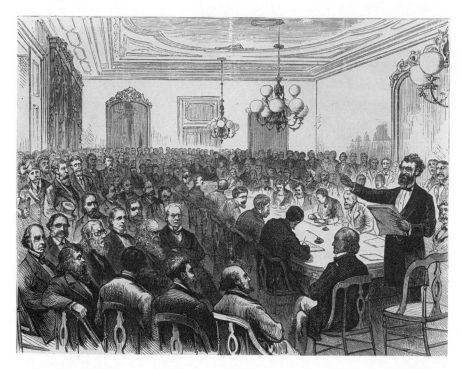

German-Americans were also active in forming the Social Democratic Party, which later became the Socialist Party of America. The first socialist elected to Congress was Victor Louis Berger, an Austrian immigrant who had settled in Wisconsin. In the 20th century, Milwaukee had a second-generation German-American, Emil Seidel, as a socialist mayor.

German-American labor groups were so large and active that several attempts were made to form a national German confederation of trade unions. But workers of all ethnic backgrounds found they needed to unite to gain basic rights. The result was the formation of the American Federation of Labor (AFL). The membership of the AFL was heavily German in the late 19th century and so was its leadership in the main industrial cities. German was often spoken in the AFL's council and committee rooms.

Most German-Americans, however, were part of the mainstream political parties. Having helped found the Republican Party, many remained active in it. Some German liberals, disgusted by corruption in Ulysses S. Grant's government, left the Republicans. Led by Carl Schurz, these liberals returned to the Democratic Party, in which other German-Americans had been active all the while.

German-Americans often mobilized politically outside major political forms, especially to fight periodic attempts to force the use of English in all schools. A number of local associations joined to form the National German-American alliance in 1901, largely around this question. By 1914, it had perhaps two million members. The use of German in the schools ceased to be an issue only after World War I.

By the end of the 20th century, the German-Americans had separated themselves into two main groups. On the one hand were the very large number who followed the advice of Carl Schurz. They gave up speaking German and belonging to specifically German organizations. Instead, they spoke, sounded, looked, and acted like any other Americans, and thought of America as their only homeland. Their numbers included many new immigrants and most second- and third-generation German Americans, that is, the children and grandchildren of immigrants. They might remember their German heritage with pleasure and affection, but they were unquestionably Americans.

On the other hand many German-Americans were German nationalists, especially (but not only) new immigrants. Many thought of themselves as both Germans *and* Americans. Especially after the rise of the German Empire, many trumpeted their pride in German military successes, technical advances, and cultural achievements. In the early 20th century, many of these people would find themselves in an agonizingly difficult position.

8

Modern Times

We are Germans, of course. I was an officer in the German Army. I have one hundred and twenty-five relatives now fighting for Germany. When people ask us, therefore, where we would stand in case of war between this country and Germany, it is like asking a man where he would stand in his own household as between his wife and his mother. However, if war ever came between this country and Germany or any other country, we would be American citizens, just as we were in the Civil War.

The Editor of the Milwaukee
Germania-Herold, *May 29, 1915*

By 1910, the U.S. Census tells us, 8,282,618 people gave Germany as their country of origin. More than two and one-half million had actually been born in Germany. The rest had one or both parents born there. Beyond these, of course, were the many millions of others whose ancestors had come from Germany decades or even centuries ago.

German communities throughout America had followed with interest and some pride Germany's unification, military success, and industrial growth. Many kept up ties with relatives and former home communities there. Some earlier emigrants had even returned home from the United States. Most, however, stayed in America and watched Germany from afar.

World War I

The outbreak of war in August 1914 came as a terrible shock to German-Americans. The United States did not actually join the British, French, and Russians in fighting the Germans and Austrians until 1917. But anti-German feeling ran strong in the country before then. German-

Americans had been proud of their contributions to the United States. Now they found themselves denounced with hatred as "Prussians," "Huns," or even "barbarians." Their clubs, schools, newspapers, churches, and associations had helped them to keep alive and enjoy their German traditions and culture. Now these were attacked as part of Germany's propaganda machine.

Many German-Americans strongly supported Germany in the European conflict. German-American newspapers did not fault Germany for causing the war. They blamed instead, as German-American historian Carl Wittke described their view, "Russia's desire for more territory; the French desire for revenge; and the British desire for profits." Many thought that England was jealous of Germany's astonishing growth in the previous decades. Many were confident that Germany, now a powerful industrial nation, would easily triumph in the war for a larger stake in Europe.

Such views were very far from those expressed in most other American papers. The United States was, from the start, neutral in law but not in spirit or action. As the war progressed, the general American press and population grew more and more sympathetic to the Allied side. As they saw it, England and its Allies were the forces of democracy, while Germany and the Axis or Central Powers were ruled by greedy, militaristic tyrants such as the German kaiser.

Many German-Americans felt that the American public was not getting the German side of the story, and undertook the job in their own papers. Sometimes they printed articles in English for their subscribers to show their English-speaking friends. A few, like New York City's *The Fatherland*, were funded by the German government. But most acted primarily from a love of their original homeland. Some German-American writers became strongly anti-British, blaming them for "poisoning" the American press against the German cause.

Lecturers, too, traveled the country, arguing the German case. German-Americans were often joined on the platform by Irish-Americans. These allies had their own anti-British sentiments, since Ireland was then attempting to win its freedom from Britain. Some Scandinavian-Americans, whose homelands had close traditional ties to Germany, also wished to avoid entering the war *against* Germany. They urged President Wilson to maintain America's officially neutral position in the war and to back away from support for the Allies.

German-Americans held huge antiwar rallies in cities all over the country, including Chicago, New York, Washington, D.C., Newark, Baltimore, Pittsburgh, Toledo, St. Louis, Philadelphia, New Orleans, Cleveland, Cincinnati, and Omaha. At one rally in Chicago of more than 10,000 people, spirits were stirred by the appearance of a parade of banner-waving German soldiers, reserves who had reported to the German consul for duty.

German-Americans also formed many relief organizations, to aid German and Austrian war casualties and their families. War bazaars and contributions made through German-American newspapers and churches raised hundreds of thousands of dollars for non-military relief. Such items as replicas of the Iron Cross, symbol of the German army, were auctioned off. Before the United States entered the war in 1917, some German war bonds were even sold in the United States.

Whether any German-Americans went beyond speechmaking and war relief to active sabotage or spying for Germany is unclear. German-Americans consistently denied that they did. But such anti-German charges were widespread throughout the United States, leading to a largely fruitless witch-hunt against German spies and saboteurs.

By 1915, the country was being warned about "hyphenated Americans"—a warning German-Americans took as an insult directed at them. Such a respected New York publication as the *Nation*—once edited by Carl Schurz—criticized "Germans who live here for convenience," commenting: "For the first time, they have raised the question of the loyalty of foreign-born citizens, not their loyalty in time of war, but that deeper, firmer, and nobler allegiance to our institutions which we have a right to expect of true Americans."

A turning point in German-American feelings toward Germany occurred in March of 1915, when a German submarine torpedoed and sank the British liner *Lusitania*, killing over 1,100 people, more than 100 of them American. Though some German-American newspapers initially greeted the sinking with pride at a German blow struck against the British, many could not in conscience justify the sinking of a civilian liner. Sadly they began to loosen their ties to the Fatherland. The editor of the St. Paul, Minnesota, *Volkszeitung* put it this way: "Whatever may be the outcome, and however painful it might be for the German-Americans, their devotion to the Stars and Stripes must never be questioned."

Even so, many German-Americans continued an active campaign for neutrality, especially in the presidential election of 1916. Democrat

Woodrow Wilson was reelected on the slogan: "He kept us out of war." But some German-Americans, unhappy with Wilson's pro-British stance, turned to the Republican Party, even though their candidate was hardly more satisfactory on the question of neutrality.

As on most other political questions, however, German-Americans differed sharply in their views. The strongest supporters of Germany against England were drawn from among those who had come most recently from Europe. Many other new immigrants supported neither side, dismayed and angry that America could let itself be drawn into one of Europe's "senseless" wars. Some German-Americans refused to send contributions to German causes, blaming the kaiser for the war.

But once America entered the war on the Allied side, most German-Americans strongly supported the American war effort, sending soldiers and buying war bonds, even those with relatives on both sides of the war. Opera star Ernestine Schumann-Heink, for example, had one son killed fighting in the Austrian army, while four other sons fought on the Allied side. An American citizen after 1908, she gave many concerts to raise funds for the Allied cause, but she refused—though strongly pressed—to condemn her Austrian son.

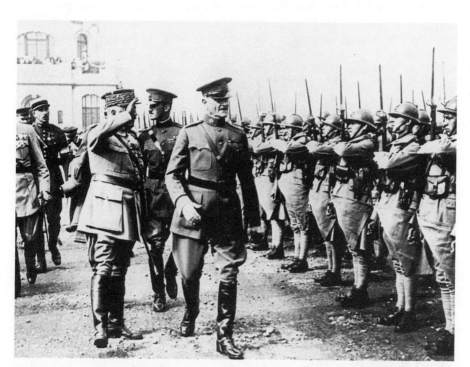

German-American General John J. Pershing, head of the American Expeditionary Force in Europe during World War 1, inspects the French guard of honor. (Photo by International, Library of Congress)

In truth, the mass of German-Americans, those who had been in the country for decades or longer, simply regarded themselves by this time as Americans. America's two greatest heroes of World War I were both of German descent—General of the Armies John J. Pershing (whose family name was originally Pfoerschin) and flying ace Captain Eddie Rickenbacker (originally Richenbacher).

Hyphenated Americans

But the pro-German views expressed in the early years of the war had created a rift between German-Americans and the rest of the American public. By 1917, when the United States entered the war on the side of the Allies, feelings against "hyphenated Americans" had bloomed into a full-blown anti-German hysteria. In some places, German-Americans were tarred and feathered, and their homes were vandalized. German towns and foods were sometimes renamed. Berlin, Iowa, became Lincoln, for example, and sauerkraut was called "liberty cabbage." Sometimes German music was banned, and German books were removed from library shelves, even publicly burned. The cartoon Katzenjammer Kids briefly had their nationality changed from German to Irish.

German-American flying ace Captain Eddie Rickenbacker, shown here in 1918 with his biplane, was one of the most acclaimed heroes of World War I. (Library of Congress)

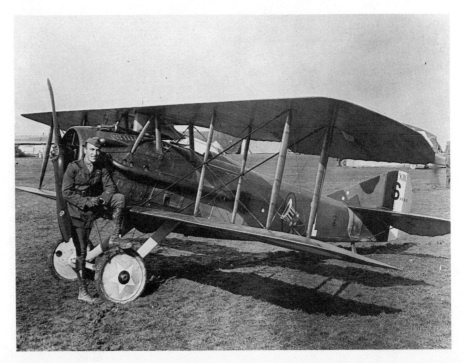

Among the hardest hit were separate German-speaking sectarian communities. During World War I, the military attempted to force pacifists to serve in the army—no conscientious objection was allowed, and people could not pay to have someone else serve in their place, as in the Civil War. Some Mennonites, Quakers, Hutterites, and other pacifists who would not fight were imprisoned under harsh conditions, and some died. Large numbers of pacifists emigrated across the border into Canada.

The teaching of German was limited or banned in many states, and some states curbed the freedom to speak German in public. The German press was sharply censored, and the number of German-language publications fell by half in just a few years. The National German-American Alliance, subject of a Senate investigation, was disbanded in April 1918. The coming of Prohibition in 1919 placed German-Americans even more at odds with many of their neighbors, many of whom supported laws against drinking.

The effects of these actions were profound. Over the centuries from their first settlement, many German-Americans had gradually Americanized their names, shortening the name, simplifying its spelling, or translating it into English. But they had kept a pride in their heritage. Now many German-Americans began to hide their names and deny their backgrounds. Many churches that had held most of their services in German now quickly switched over to using English, and parochial schools did the same. German-Americans who had hesitated to enter the mainstream now dove in and became no longer hyphenated Americans but simply Americans.

To some extent this simply speeded up a process that was taking place in any case, since the main language for most young German-Americans was now English. Over the decades the shift to English would be almost complete, except for the tens of thousands of sectarians still living in closed communities, some of whom believe that German is the only proper language of their religion. Among these are groups like the Hutterites, the Amish, and other sectarians, who remain in Pennsylvania and several other states.

Between the Wars

While German-Americans were merging almost completely into the American background, they continued to make major political and cultural contributions to the life of the land.

In the literary world, American-born H.L. (Henry Louis) Mencken had become a well-known journalist on the Baltimore *Sun* even before the war. After it he produced his major three-volume work, *The American Language*, a still-unmatched look at the background and the character of modern American English. In private letters to German-American friends, H.L. sometimes jokingly referred to himself as "Heinrich Ludwig." One of these friends was German-American Theodore Dreiser, author of the great American novels *Sister Carrie* and *An American Tragedy*. Dreiser's brother, Paul Dresser, wrote some of the most popular songs of early 20th-century America, including "My Gal Sal" and "On the Banks of the Wabash Far Away," still the state song of Indiana.

The folk tales collected in early 19th-century Germany by the brothers Jakob and Wilhelm Grimm began to circulate widely in English translation. This brought into the American world characters like Hansel and Gretel, Little Red Riding Hood, Snow White, Rumpelstiltskin, and Sleeping Beauty. German-Americans Edward Stratemeyer and his daughter, Harriet, writing as Carolyn Keene, began to create a whole string of popular children's books, featuring amateur detective Nancy Drew and the Hardy Boys, as well as the Bobbsey twins and Tom Swift. Later in the century, German-Dutch-American John Steinbeck was awarded the Nobel Prize for his novels, among them *Grapes of Wrath*, *East of Eden*, and *Of Mice and Men*. Another great American novelist of German background was Thomas Wolfe, whose *You Can't Go Home Again* and *Look Homeward, Angel* drew on his early life in Asheville, North Carolina.

German-Americans continued to be active in classical music in all its forms. German popular music also was widespread. In the late 19th and early 20th century, German street bands earned a little money from passersby as they strolled about cities. Revived after World War II, many amateur or semiprofessional bands play popular German—mostly Bavarian—style music at fests and festivals around the country. German instruments and popular music have to some extent become part of American popular music, through people like German-American Lawrence Welk. They also form part of America's regional music, as the accordion and polka rhythms of Texas German music have mixed with other ethnic music of the region to form the music style today called zydeco.

In the musical theater, the great showman Florenz Ziegfeld (son of a Chicago German music teacher) created a series of revues—combining songs, comic routines, and dance numbers involving dozens of beautiful women—called the Ziegfeld Follies. Until his death in 1932, Ziegfeld's shows were the toast of Broadway, creating dozens of stars. Other German-Americans helped create the Broadway musical comedy, a unique blend of the old world operetta and American popular entertainment forms. Among them were Oscar Hammerstein II (grandson of the opera owner), who with Richard Rodgers created *Oklahoma!* and *South Pacific*, among other musicals.

In the movies, Irish-German-American Walt Disney's animated films gave new life to many of the old German folk-tale characters, such as Snow White. Mary Astor, who so memorably played Brigid O'Shaughnessy in *The Maltese Falcon*, was a German-American born Lucile Langhanke. Johnny Weissmuller, son of a Viennese brewmaster, was Hollywood's most popular Tarzan. Fred Astaire, dancer extraordinaire and model of sophistication, was the son of a German-born Kansas brewer named Austerlitz. Millions of people learned to dance through the dance studios of Austrian-American Arthur Murray.

In sports, German-Americans made gymnastics popular and contributed many excellent players to team sports such as baseball and football. Two of the most famous are baseball greats Babe (George

Always music lovers, many German immigrants in the late 19th century formed street bands, like this one in New York City. (By J.G. Brown, Harper's Weekly, April 26, 1879)

Herman Erhardt) Ruth and Lou Gehrig. These two players were occasionally found talking German to each other, and to German-American sports writers, off the field. Another German-American baseball player, Peter (Honus) Wagner, had a batting average even higher than the Babe's. German-American Gertrude Ederle was the first woman to swim the English Channel, and beat the record of the men who had done so before her.

In 1920 German-American Harry Burt put chocolate-covered ice cream on a stick and created an American institution—the Good Humor Ice Cream Sucker—sold from a visiting truck with bells to alert eager buyers. German immigrant Gayelord Hauser made a career of writing and lecturing about health food. German immigrant Charles Nestle, born Karl Ludwig Nessler, introduced the "permanent wave" to American beauty parlors in 1915. And a Viennese cosmetics formula was the basis for Estée Lauder's highly successful company.

German-Americans and new immigrants alike began to move into the political mainstream, too. German-Jewish-American Felix Frankfurter, who came to the United States in 1894 and attended Harvard University, was appointed to the Supreme Court in 1939. German-born Robert Ferdinand Wagner, arriving in America a poor eight-year-old boy in 1885, became a powerful U.S. senator, helping to shape the legislation of the New Deal, especially the National Labor Relations Board. His son, Robert F. Wagner, Jr., was an influential three-term mayor of New York City. Though most German-Americans were proud of being law-abiding citizens, some among them took a different turn, such as the notorious gangster Dutch Schultz, born Arthur Flegenheimer.

Nazis in America

After the World War I hysteria had passed away, German-Americans founded some other organizations, such as the Steuben Society, aiming to promote positive views of the German heritage and defend German-Americans from attack. But they never attracted wide membership. The mass of German-Americans was now firmly in the mainstream.

Not surprisingly, then, when the German Nazi Party began trying to recruit members in America in 1924, they had little success. In fact, most of their recruits came from among immigrants who had come from

Germany after World War I. An early American Nazi group called the Friends of New Germany disbanded in 1935 after investigation by the House of Representatives. German-born Fritz Julius Kuhn, head of the Detroit branch of the Friends, then founded a new group: the German-American People's League, better known as the German-American Bund. This group got a great deal of attention from street rallies during the Depression in industrial cities like New York. But even the Bund never had more than 25,000 actual members, and only about 10 percent of them were American-born or had lived in America before 1900. Also investigated by the House of Representatives, the German-American Bund (weakened in any case by Kuhn's stealing of funds) was dissolved when the United States entered World War II.

Many German-American leaders and publishers at first tried to avoid the Nazi question. But by 1938, embarrassed by the racism and hatred of the Nazis, they had generally come to condemn both the Bund and Hitler's Germany. Only a few, such as German-born Georg Sylvester Viereck, continued to support the German position in books and pamphlets, as he had for decades. Many German-Americans were isolationists—that is, they would like to have kept America out of the war, until it was inevitable. But there was certainly no repeat of the pro-German support seen before World War I.

Refugees from Hitler

Meanwhile the small number of American Nazis was being overshadowed by the large number of refugees from Nazi Germany. Like some of the earliest religious dissenters and the Forty-Eighters, these new immigrants had generally given up hope of change in their homeland. They had not done so lightly. Some had gone first to other parts of Europe hoping to wait out a "temporary storm." Only after Hitler's Nazis took full hold did they make a permanent move, often to America.

Many of these refugees were older people who emigrated with their families. They had no desire to create a "new Germany" in America. They prized the freedom and democracy that America offered. At the same time, they were proud of their German heritage, and sharply distinguished between the Nazis and the German people. A few felt so strongly about their homeland that, after the war, they returned to help rebuild

Germany. Most stayed, however. Many of these new immigrants made enormous contributions to 20th-century America, a young, still-growing country.

Some of the best-known of the German refugees of this period are musicians. Vienna-born Kurt Adler, who arrived in America in 1938, became director of the Chicago, San Francisco, and then New York Metropolitan operas. Violinist and teacher Adolf Busch, leader of the great Busch quartet, came in the same year. His son-in-law, Rudolf Serkin, and grandson, Peter Serkin, both pianists, continue the family's musical traditions in America. After arriving in 1937 Viennese Erich Leinsdorf worked as a conductor in New York, Los Angeles, Cleveland, Rochester, and Boston, with time off for service in the American army during World War II. Composing giant Arnold Schönberg, also from Vienna, lived the last 17 years of his life in America. Berlin-born Bruno Walter (born Schlesinger) had conducted in America many times before he fled Germany and became an American citizen. Schönberg and Walter both settled in California, as an increasing number of modern German immigrants would do.

The von Trapp Family Singers, immortalized in the movie The Sound of Music, *are shown at a performace in Washington, shortly after they had fled Nazi-ruled Austria.* (Copyright *Washington Post*; reprinted by permission of the D.C. Public Library)

Kurt Weill, who composed *Threepenny Opera* in Germany, came to America in 1935, with his wife, Lotte Lenya, the star of the musical. In this country, Weill created many Broadway musicals, including *Knickerbocker Holiday* and *Lady in the Dark*. The great producer-director Max Reinhardt also enriched the American theater. The von Trapp family, popular singers in Europe, fled from Nazi-held Austria and settled in America. Their life and experiences inspired the movie, *The Sound of Music*. Billy Wilder, who later directed the classic films *Sunset Boulevard* and *Some Like It Hot*, and Otto Preminger, director of *Stalag 17* and *Laura*, also arrived in this period. So did Paul Henreid, born Paul von Hernreid, famous for portraying Ingrid Bergman's husband in *Casablanca*, and actor-director Erich von Stroheim. They joined many other actors and directors who had come somewhat earlier, among them Marlene Dietrich and her manager-director, Josef von Sternberg.

Several German-born and -trained architects had an enormous impact on modern American architecture. Prime among them were Walter Gropius at Harvard University and Ludwig Mies van der Rohe at Chicago's Armour Institute (now the Illinois Institute of Technology). In training some of America's most influential architects, they helped shape the cityscape of modern America. Later, German immigrant Peter Max created the psychedelic poster look that marked 1960s popular art.

Writers and professors, too, fled Germany, among them theologian Paul Tillich; philosopher Ernst Cassirer; political scientist John Neumann; music critic Alfred Einstein; art critic Erwin Panofsky; Rudolf Flesch, librarian and author of *Why Johnny Can't Read*; and historian Hajo Holborn, whose daughter, Hanna Holborn Gray, became president of Hunter College and the University of Chicago. In art, the most prominent German immigrant was painter Josef Albers. Albers and many other less famous artists often worked in progressive settings such as Black Mountain College in North Carolina. Many other writers and thinkers found work in universities and colleges across the country, where they had a powerful influence on generations of students.

American science and technology were also enormously enriched by this wave of illustrious immigrants. Perhaps the most famous of all German immigrants in the Hitler period is physicist Albert Einstein. Discoverer of the principle of relativity, he was an internationally acclaimed figure by the time he arrived, and his work laid the basis for the atomic age. Einstein spent most of his later years working at the Princeton University Institute for Advanced Study. But he also was a figure of great humanity. His

Many refugees from Hitler's Germany became American citizens as soon as they had been here long enough to do so. Here the great physicist Albert Einstein takes the oath of citizenship, along with his daughter and his secretary.
(National Archives)

thoughts on peace and brotherhood spoke to millions of people to whom his famous equation $E = mc^2$ meant nothing.

Others less well-known to the public came too. Mathematician Richard Courant, removed from his professorship in Germany, came to teach thousands of American students, building the country's prime institute of applied mathematics and making a major contribution to World War II. Four refugee scientists, including Einstein, were already Nobel Prize winners. Many others were later awarded the Nobel Prize for their work in the United States. Among these was Hans Bethe, from Strasbourg, who served as head of theoretical physics when the first atom bomb was being built. In fact, the Americans might well have not been able to build the bomb—or at least do so before the Germans—without the work of German refugee scientists. J. Robert Oppenheimer, son of a German immigrant, headed the project.

German, especially Austrian, psychologists also had a major impact on modern America, bringing various schools of psychological thought from Vienna, especially Freud's psychotherapy and Gestalt therapy. German refugees made major contributions in other sciences as well, notably in the exploration of DNA, carrier of the secrets of life, and in the study of nerve regeneration. Many scientists migrated to the fast-growing universities of California.

In addition to these well-known German refugees came many other people from all walks of life. They arrived in America at a difficult time, in the midst of a Depression, often knowing little or no English. Some had few skills, others had degrees in areas such as medicine or law that did not allow them to practice here. That sometimes meant years of work at unskilled or semi-skilled jobs, such as dishwashing or gardening, while they learned the language and then went through their many years of schooling again in America.

The War and After

By 1941, the earlier German-Americans and the new German immigrants had so completely cut their ties with Germany that America's entry into the war did not cause massive new anti-German protests. German-born residents had to register as "enemy aliens," though, and many who were eligible quickly became American citizens. There were occasional charges and a few cases of German-Americans spying for Germany, but on the whole German-Americans had come to be regarded as they had come to see themselves—as simply Americans.

That does not mean that the coming of another war with Germany was not painful. Many German-Americans still had close relatives living in Europe. Talking privately, many of them wondered if they might be fighting or even killing a cousin at the front. But fight they did, without reservation, on both the European and Pacific fronts.

How thoroughly the German-Americans had come to be blended into the American population is shown by the fact that the commander-in-chief of all the Allied operations in Europe was an American of German descent: General Dwight David Eisenhower. No one could have fought harder. (Surprisingly, he was the child of pacifists, whose Mennonite ancestors had come to Pennsylvania in the mid-1700s.) It was Eisenhower who demanded unconditional surrender of German forces, who refused even to meet with any German leaders until the surrender documents had been signed, and who forced German townspeople to walk through the horrible Nazi death camps to see how their government had killed millions of Jews, Poles, Gypsies, and political and religious dissenters. Never did the

Dwight D. Eisenhower, shown here talking to paratroopers just before the June 6, 1944, invasion of German-held France, was Supreme Allied Commander in Europe during World War II—although his German-American family had, for centuries, been pacifists.
(Library of Congress)

freedoms of America and the protections of its democratic Constitution seem sweeter.

In the years after the war, still more refugees came, for the doors were for a time thrown open wider to Europe's "orphans of the storm." Among the new German immigrants were well over 100 key scientists and technicians, especially rocket experts. (Some of these, the public learned only decades later, had actually been strong Nazi supporters, which the United States recruiters ignored in their eagerness to gain their expertise for America.) Prime among these rocket experts was Wernher von Braun, whose father had served in the government of the short-lived Weimar Republic. During the war, von Braun had developed the famous V-2 rockets, used to bomb England. These recruited scientists formed the core of the space team that took Americans to the moon and beyond.

Another prominent refugee from Germany after the war was Henry Kissinger. Arriving at age 15, he won highest honors at Harvard and, after taking his Ph.D., remained there to teach. A chief foreign policy advisor to President Richard Nixon, Kissinger helped reopen relations between America and mainland China. He became secretary of state in

1973, and that same year was awarded the Nobel Peace Prize for helping to end the war in Vietnam.

Viennese Bruno Bettelheim survived the Nazi death camps. In this country he has done important work in child psychology, especially in the treatment of autistic (severely withdrawn) children.

Many of these and other postwar refugees quickly became Americanized, adopting the language, dress, and life-style of their neighbors. As many people after the war began moving from the cities into the suburbs, so did German-Americans. No longer did even the new immigrants huddle together in a "Little Germany." With the Americanization of both old and new German-Americans, many of the remaining German organizations and publications began to die out. In the mid-1970s, only two dozen German-language publications remained in the country, where once there had been ten times that many or more. Social clubs, singing societies, and all kinds of special German organizations continued the sharp decline that had started after World War I. In Chicago, for example, the number of singing societies dropped from 200 in 1900 to 95 in 1935 to just 10 in the mid-1970s.

German-Americans continued to contribute to American life. Novelist Kurt Vonnegut, Jr., drew on his experiences as a prisoner of war in a German camp for his novel *Slaughterhouse Five*. Dr. Seuss (actually a German-American named Theodore Geisel) created his wonderful

In the 1970s, German-born Henry Kissinger (left) was a major foreign policy advisor to President Richard Nixon (right), and helped bring about the end of the Vietnam War and the reopening of relations with China. (Copyright Washington Post; *reprinted by permission of the D.C. Public Library)*

children's books, including *The Cat in the Hat* and *The Grinch That Stole Christmas*. Cartoonist Charles Schulz created the unforgettable Snoopy, Lucy, Linus, and the well-known "security blanket." German-Swedish-American Hugh Hefner helped create new attitudes about sexual relations with his magazine *Playboy*, beginning in 1953. William P. Lear developed his corporate jets—and also the eight-track stereo cartridge.

New Relationships

In the years after the war, America moved into a very different relationship with Germany. Under the Marshall Plan, massive amounts of money and expert aid were sent to help rebuild West Germany, which had been bombed to rubble. As the Cold War began, pitting East against West, West Germany became an important ally of the West, while East Germany was part of the Communist bloc. American soldiers stationed in Germany and German civilians came to know each other better and better—enough so that a large number of modern German immigrants are women who have married American soldiers stationed in Germany. Today West Germany has a very strong economy, testimony to the continuing hard work and technical expertise of Germans, and has become one of America's major allies and trading partners.

Though revulsion still remains for the actions of the Nazis during World War II, that feeling generally does not extend to German people and customs in America. Quite the contrary. Old-style German communities, as in the Pennsylvania Dutch country, and museums or restorations, such as the old Moravian settlement at Salem, North Carolina, have become increasingly popular tourist sites, reminders of America's colonial past. People around the country enjoy German-style celebrations, such as "Oktoberfests," where musicians and dancers dress up in Bavarian folk costumes and play "oompah" music. Many of the entertainers and audience have little or no German ancestry. They simply enjoy the bouncy music, friendly beer drinking, and joyous dancing found at German-American social gatherings. And many people who celebrate "German Day" or "Steuben Day" with an autumn parade are not necessarily German, but appreciate the enormous contribution the German-Americans have made to their adopted country.

Today German-Americans have blended almost completely into the American mainstream. Two American presidents were German-

Today people all over the country, whether or not they have German ancestry, enjoy attending Mayfests and Oktoberfests, where they are entertained by "oompah" bands and Bavarian-style dancers like these. (Copyright *Washington Post*; reprinted by permission of the D.C. Public Library)

Americans—Herbert Hoover and Dwight David Eisenhower. Two others, William McKinley and Lyndon Johnson, were partly of German descent. But all four were seen simply as "American." The same is true of Warren Burger, former chief justice of the Supreme Court; former vice president and New York State governor Nelson D. Rockefeller; and Fredericksburg, Texas, native Admiral Chester Nimitz, commander of the Pacific Fleet and later head of naval operations during World War II.

In *Beyond the Melting Pot*, Nathan Glazer and Daniel P. Moynihan put it this way: "While German influence is to be seen in virtually every aspect of the city's [New York] life, the Germans as a group are vanished. No appeals are made to the German vote, there are no German politicians in the sense that there are Irish and Italian politicians . . ." They call it a case of "ethnic disappearance." The same is true around the country almost everywhere that Germans have settled.

Yet, as Glazer and Moynihan pointed out, their influence *is* all around us. Many German contributions—from the hamburger and the frankfurter to the Christmas tree and the Easter bunny, from graduate schools and the Good Humor man to the Republican elephant and the Democratic donkey—have today been so widely accepted as to seem utterly American.

As for the German-Americans themselves, new and old they still appreciate the freedom and opportunity that America has to offer.

German-born Arno Penzias, winner of the 1978 Nobel Prize for Physics, put it this way:

> My mother was a cleaning woman and our family wasn't able to live too well. Now I have as many suits as my closet can hold. I've won the Nobel Prize. Many people are saying the American Dream no longer is a reality today. Well, I've realized it. The American Dream has come true for me.

Suggestions for
Further Reading

Abbott, Edith. *Immigration: Select Documents and Case Records*. New York: Arno, 1969.

Bailyn, Bernard. *The Peopling of British North America*, Vol. 1: *An Introduction*. Vol. 2: *Voyagers to the West: A Passage in the Peopling of America on the Eve of Revolution*. New York: Knopf, 1986.

Bernardo, Stephanie. *The Ethnic Almanac*. Garden City, New York: Doubleday (Dolphin), 1981.

Billigmeier, Robert Henry. *Americans From Germany: A Study in Cultural Diversity*. Belmont, California: Wadsworth, 1974. Part of the Minorities in American Life series.

Bittinger, Lucy Forney. *The Germans in Colonial Times*. Philadelphia: Lippincott, 1901; reprint New York: Russell & Russell (Atheneum), 1968.

Brownstone, David M. *The Jewish-American Heritage*. New York: Facts On File, 1988. Part of the America's Ethnic Heritage series.

——, Irene M. Franck, and Douglass L. Brownstone. *Island of Hope, Island of Tears*. New York: Rawson, Wade, 1979; New York: Viking-Penguin, 1986.

Coser, Lewis A. *Refugee Scholars in America: Their Impact and Their Experiences*. New Haven, Connecticut: Yale University Press, 1984.

Diamond, Sander A. *The Nazi Movement in the United States, 1924-1941*. Ithaca, New York: Cornell University Press, 1974.

Dobbert, Guido A. "German-Americans between New and Old Fatherland, 1870-1914." *American Quarterly* 19 (1967): 663-680

Faust, Albert Bernhardt. *The German Element in the United States, with Special Reference to Its Political, Moral, Social, and Educational Influence*, in two vols. Boston: Houghton, Mifflin, 1909; reprint in one volume, New York: Steuben Society of America, 1927 (revised through 1917).

Fermi, Laura. *Illustrious Immigrants: The Intellectual Migration from Europe, 1930-41*, second edition. Chicago: University of Chicago Press, 1971.

Franck, Irene M., and David M. Brownstone. *To the Ends of the Earth*. New York: Facts On File, 1984.

The German Reich and Americans of German Origin. New York: Oxford University Press, 1938.

Goldmark, Josephine. *Pilgrims of '48: One Man's Part in the Austrian Revolution of 1848 and a Family Migration to America*. New Haven, Connecticut: Yale University Press, 1930.

Handlin, Oscar. *A Pictorial History of Immigration*. New York: Crown, 1972.

Hansen, Marcus Lee. *The Atlantic Migration: 1607-1860: A History of the Continuing Settlement of the United States*. Cambridge, Massachusetts: Harvard University Press, 1945.

Hawgood, John. *The Tragedy of German-America: The Germans in the United States during the Nineteenth Century and After*. New York: Putnam, 1940.

Heilbut, Anthony. *Exiled in Paradise: German Refugee Artists and Intellectuals in America, from the 1930's to the Present*. New York: Viking, 1983.

Holborn, Hajo. *A History of Modern Germany*, in three volumes. New York: Knopf. Vol. I: *The Reformation*. 1949. Vol. II: *1648-1840*. 1971. Vol III: *1840-1945*. 1969.

Hostetler, John A. *Amish Society*. Baltimore: Johns Hopkins Press, 1963.

Jones, Maldwyn Allen. *American Immigration*. Chicago: University of Chicago Press, 1960.

———. *Destination America*. New York: Holt, Rinehart, and Winston, 1976.

Klees, Frederic. *The Pennsylvania Dutch*. New York: Macmillan, 1950.

Knittle, Walter A. *Early Eighteenth Century Palatine Emigration*. Philadelphia: Dorrance, 1937; reprint Baltimore, Genealogical Publishing, 1965.

Köllman, Wolfgang, and Peter Marshalck. "German Emigration to the United States," *Perspectives in American History* 7 (1973): 499-557.

Kunz, Virginia Brainard. *The Germans in America*. Minneapolis: Lerner, 1966. Part of the In America series.

Low, Alfred D. *Jews in the Eyes of the Germans: From the Enlightenment to Imperial Germany*. Philadelphia: Institute for the Study of Human Issues, 1979.

Luebke, Frederick C. *Bonds of Loyalty: German-Americans and World War I*. Northern Illinois University Press: De Kalb, 1974.

Miller, Sally M. *The Radical Immigrant*. New York: Twayne, 1974. Part of the Immigrant Heritage of America series.

Miller, Wayne Charles. *A Comprehensive Bibliography for the Study of American Minorities*, in two vols. New York: New York University Press, 1976.

Mittelberger, Gottlieb. *Journey to Pennsylvania*. Oscar Handlin and John Clives, eds. and trans. Cambridge, Massachusetts: Belknap Press of Harvard University Press, 1960.

The Muses Flee Hitler: Cultural Transfer and Adaptation, 1930-1945. Smithsonian, 1983.

Neidle, Cecyle S. *America's Immigrant Women*. Boston: Twayne (G.K. Hall), 1975. Part of the Immigrant Heritage of America Series.

Norwood, Frederick A. *Strangers and Exiles: A History of Religious Refugees*, in two volumes. Nashville, Abingdon: 1969.

Novotny, Ann. *Strangers at the Door: Ellis Island, Castle Garden, and the Great Migration to America*. Riverside, Connecticut: Chatham, 1971.

O'Connor, Richard. *The German-Americans: An Informal History*. Boston: Little, Brown, 1968.

Parsons, William T. *The Pennsylvania Dutch: A Persistent Minority*. Boston: Twayne (G.K. Hall), 1976. Part of the Immigrant Heritage of America series.

Pfanner, Helmut F. *Exile in New York: German and Austrian Writers after 1933*. Wayne, Nebraska: Wayne State University Press, 1983.

Rickett, Richard. *A Brief Survey of Austrian History*. Wien (Vienna): George Prachner Verlag, 1968.

Rippley, LaVern J. *The German-Americans*. Boston: Twayne, 1976. Part of the Immigrant Heritage of America series.

————. *Of German Ways*. Minneapolis: Dillon, 1970; reprint New York: Gramercy, 1986.

Robbins, Albert. *Coming to America: Immigrants from Northern Europe*. New York: Delacorte, 1981. Part of the Coming to America series.

Taylor, Philip. *The Distant Magnet*. New York: Harper and Row, 1972.

Thernstrom, Stephan, ed. *Harvard Encyclopedia of American Ethnic Groups*. Cambridge, Massachusetts: Belknap Press of the Harvard University Press, 1980.

Trommler, Frank, and Joseph McVeigh, eds. *America and the Germans: An Assessment of a Three-Hundred-Year History*, in 2 volumes. Vol. I: *Immigration, Language, Ethnicity*. Vol. II: *The Relationship in the*

Twentieth Century. Philadelphia: University of Pennsylvania Press, 1985.

Walker, Mack. *Germany and the Emigration, 1816-1885*. Cambridge, Massachusetts: Harvard University Press, 1964.

Wandel, Joseph. *The German Dimension of American History*. Chicago: Nelson-Hall, 1979.

Wittke, Carl. *German-Americans and the World War: (With Special Emphasis on Ohio's German-Language Press)*. Columbus, Ohio: The Ohio State Archaeological and Historical Society, 1936. Reprint Jerome S. Ozer, 1974, part of the United States in World War series.

————. *Refugees of Revolution: The German Forty-Eighters in America*. Philadelphia: University of Pennsylvania Press, 1952.

————. *We Who Built America: The Saga of the Immigrant*. New York: Prentice-Hall, 1939; reprint, Cleveland: The Press of Case Western Reserve University, 1964.

Wood, Ralph, ed. *The Pennsylvania Germans*. Princeton, New Jersey: Princeton University Press, 1942.

Zucker, Adolf E., ed. *The Forty-Eighters: Political Refugees of the German Revolution of 1848*. New York: Columbia University Press, 1950; reprint New York: Russell & Russell, 1967.

INDEX